Marble and Stone Slab Veneer

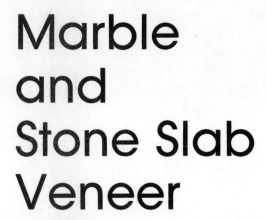

James E. Amrhein, S.E.

Executive Director

Michael W. Merrigan

Staff Engineer

Masonry Institute of America

2550 Beverly Boulevard

Los Angeles, CA 90057

Published by
Masonry Institute of America
Los Angeles, California 90057

ISBN 0-940116-15-4
Printed in the United States of America
MIA 511 : 5-86 : 4M
MIA 511 : 3-89 : 5M

This publication was prepared in keeping with current information and practice for
the present state-of-the-art of veneer and dimensional stone slab design and construction. This publication expresses the opinions of the authors, and care has
been taken to ensure that all data and information furnished are as accurate as
possible. Although they have endeavored to supplement this data by conferences
with experts and have obtained qualified advice, the authors and the publisher
cannot assume nor accept any responsibility or liability (including liability for
negligence) for possible errors or oversights in this data and information and in
the use of such information or in the preparation of plans or details.

Contents

Preface

Throughout the years, building stone has been used for artistic expression. Limited only by the imagination of the designer who wants the artistic features and permanence of building stone, these features are obtained through the assemblage of essential pieces into a magnificent sculpture of a building.

The scope of this publication is to assist in the design of details in building stone facades. It is intended to show standard details and, recognizing that each project presents different design facets, each of the details should be reviewed and adapted to each specific design.

The selection and adaptation of the proper, simple connections, anchors and explicit details will greatly ensure that fabrication and installation will be made with the minimum of problems.

This publication has been developed to assist the designer who uses natural thin stone slab veneer.

The authors recommend quickly reading through the book from cover to cover. This will not take much time since the book is not very long or difficult. This quick read-through will alert the reader of what is available. It will certainly stimulate new ideas for the designer.

The Masonry Institute of America

The Masonry Institute of America, founded in 1957 under the name Masonry Research, is a professional promotion, technical and research organization established to improve and extend the uses of masonry. It is supported by the mason contractors through a labor management contract between the unions and contractors. The Masonry Institute of America is active in Los Angeles County of California in promoting new ideas and masonry work, improving building codes, conducting research, presenting design, construction and inspection seminars, and writing technical and non-technical papers, all for the purpose of improving the masonry industry. The Masonry Institute of America does not compete with architects or engineers in design or in bidding, contracting or supervision of masonry construction.

Acknowledgements

The authors greatly appreciate the assistance afforded by Carrara Marble Company of America, Inc. We are particularly appreciative of Robert Price, Vice President in charge of Field Operations, who provided a great deal of practical advice and helped assure the accuracy of this publication. We are indebted to Gary Swieso, Project Officer, for his advice on marble applications and to Frederick Cordova, Chief Executive Officer, and William Cordova, President, who were very supportive of our many requests from their company and quite helpful in reviewing the manuscript.

The manual *Marble Design II* by Marble Institute of America was used as a reference for portions of this book.

The authors also acknowledge J. William Minkler, President of California Marble Co./Multi-Seal Pacific Corp., for his valuable assistance with the section on Cleaning, Waterproofing and Protection.

The assistance of Chang M. Ahn, Hien (Helen) Le Vuong, and Minh Thanh Ngo, drafts persons who drew the details, is appreciated.

The authors express their appreciation for the cooperation and assistance of the many other people who aided in the preparation of this manuscript.

1
Introduction

Man has had an enduring relationship with stone since he first used caves for shelter.

The development of stone in construction has been a continually evolving process. Stone was first used for shelter simply because it formed the walls of the caves in which early man hid from the ravages of the elements. This worked, but early man had to leave the shelter of his dark cave to forage and hunt. Later, as man evolved, he used large, solid blocks of stone to build his home where and how he wanted. This worked better. Now the home could be built closer to food and water and also be built with a greater degree of comfort. Unfortunately, building with solid stone was a costly venture requiring much time and labor. Only the very wealthy could build with stone.

Today we use thin slabs of natural stone to clad our buildings in aesthetically pleasing stone veneer. Now any building can be economically built with stone.

Some of the features of stone construction are its natural beauty, the subliminal feeling of security, and eternal strength that it creates. In addition, marble and granite do not lose their beauty with age as do so many other materials. Marble and granite age gracefully with the passing years and weather nature's fury with a serenity that befits one of man's earliest means of shelter.

1.1 General Information on Stone

Natural stone, such as marble and granite, is the most beautiful of earth's natural materials used in construction. The variegated surface of marble and the visual strength of granite have made these stones ideal for the creative designer.

1.1.1 Geological Classification

The rocks that form the earth's crust fall into three genetic groups:

- Igneous
- Sedimentary
- Metamorphic

When the earth formed, the crust was at one stage a viscous liquid skin that slowly cooled and hardened into igneous rock. Granite is a multicolored intrusive igneous rock ranging in color from white through black.

Granite is composed of quartz, feldspar, mica, and sometimes ferro magnesium minerals. As igneous rock weathers, it deteriorates into deposited soils that then consolidate due to heat, pressure, and cementation to produce sedimentary rock.

Sedimentary rocks are also formed by the process of cementing, consolidating crystalization and hardening of chemical solutions and biological deposits.

When sedimentary rocks are subjected to increasing heat, pressure, and shear, the minerals are then altered chemically and distorted or physically realigned to produce metamorphic rocks. These new rocks may resemble their original ancestors but are usually more crystaline and denser. Igneous rocks may also be metamorphosed by heat, pressure, and shear, but the changes are usually less drastic.

It is in this manner that metamorphic rocks are formed, differing widely from the igneous or sedimentary types and being usually much denser than either. When limestones or dolomites crystalize, they form a metamorphic rock commonly called marble. All calcereous rocks as well as some dolomitic and serpentine rocks that are able to be polished are commercially called marbles.

Table 1.1 shows various physical properties and characteristics of building stone.

1.2 Texture of Quarried Stone

The term ''texture,'' as applied to marble, relates to the size, shape, degree of uniformity and arrangement of the component grains or crystals. The texture, or grain pattern, can be:

EQUIGRANULAR—grains of approximately the same size, such as limestone;

INEQUIGRANULAR—grains of markedly unequal sizes, such as granite;

PORPHYRITIC—relatively large, course crystals, called phenocrysts, of one or more mineral components in a ground mass of markedly finer texture, such as granite;

INTERLOCKING—where grains with irregular boundaries interlock by mutual penetration, such as granite and breccia;

MOSAIC (or GRANULITIC)—closely packed grains with smooth to moderately irregular, non-interlocking mutual boundaries, such as feldspar and pyroxene;

ELASTIC—naturally cemented fragmental grains but without interlocking or mosaic relations, such as quartzite;

GRANO BLASTIC—a granular mosaic texture in which the grains are tightly compacted, the minerals are dominantly of equidimensional kinds and present irregular mutual boundaries, such as granitte.

The main components of most marbles are grains of crystalline calcite with definite cleavage planes which when broken show bright reflecting surfaces. In most marbles, however, the grains are elongated in one direction by the folding of the beds.

Any interlocking grain texture is typified by granite and other granitoid rocks.

1.3 Classification of Fabricated Stone for Soundness

The Marble Institute of America has classified marble into four groups. These classifications of marble are based on the typical characteristics that may be found during fabrication. This classification does not attempt to rate stones as to their quality. The groupings merely indicate the level of fabrication considered necessary and acceptable in each group.

Classification of marble is done by the producer and finisher. Producers and finishers should provide written warranties before installation is begun.

The groupings—A, B, C and D—should be taken into account when specifying marble and stone, for not all stones are suitable for building applications. The marbles in groups C and D are more fragile than those found in groups A and B. Group C and D marbles may require extra fabrication effort before or during installation. Granite and the four marble groups are defined as follows:

GRANITE—Granite and very sound stones with uniform and very favorable working qualities.

GROUP A—Marbles and stones unimpaired by weakened planes with very little variation in fabrication quality.

GROUP B—Marbles and stones with a nature similar to the preceding group. Working qualities are somewhat less favorable. Stones in this group may have natural faults requiring some waxing and sticking.

GROUP C—Marbles and stones with even greater variations in working qualities; natural flaws, voids, stains and lines of separation are more common. These variations in the stone are usually repaired before installation by sticking, waxing and filling the voids. When necessary, liners, strong backs or other forms of reinforcement are used.

GROUP D—Marble and stone similar to the preceding group but containing a larger proportion of natural faults and a maximum variation in working qualities, requiring more of the same methods of finishing. Many of the more variegated marbles fit into this group.

1.3.1 Travertine

Some travertine stone that take a polish are classified as marble, according to ASTM C119. Travertine is actually a variety of limestone regarded as a product of chemical precipitation from hot springs. This results in a cellular stone with the cells usually concentrated in thin layers that display a stalactic structure.

Table 1.1 Physical Properties and Characteristics of Stone

CHARACTERISTICS	GRANITE	TRAP-ROCK "Black Granite"	LIMESTONE			SANDSTONE		
			Low Density	Medium Density	High Density	Sandstone	Quartzitic Sandstone	Quartzite
GEOLOGY	Igneous	Igneous	Sedimentary			Sedimentary		
MINEROLOGY	Quartz, Alkalie, Feldspar	Pyroxene, Hornblend, biotite	Calcite, Dolomite			Quartz, Feldspar		
CHEMISTRY (approximate composition)	70% SiO_2 15% Al_2O_3		50% to 97% $CaCO_3$ 2% to 50% $MgCO_3$			$SiO^2\,NaAlS_3^3\,O_8$ $KAls_1^2O_8CaAlS_{13}^3\,O_8$		
GEOGRAPHY	MA, NH, VT, RI, CT, NY, NJ, MD, VA, NC, SC, GA, WI, MN, MO, OK, TX, CA, SD, ME, PA	Pink Green Blue Black	NY to AL, IN to MS, IA, NE, KA, MO, OK, AR, TX, WI, CO, SD, WY, CA, MN			Most States		
COLORS	Pink, Brown, Gray, White, Blue, Black, Green, Red	Pink Green Blue Black	White, Cream, Gray, Rust, Pink, Black, Buff, Tan, Ivory, Blue, Rose			Brown, Gray, Rose, Cream, Buff, Ivory, Pink, Tan, Yellow, Beige, White, Red, Gold, Purple, Blue, Rust		
SIZE MAXIMUM ft² ASTM specification	75 C615–80	— —	70 C568–79			C616–80		
DENSITY, lbs/ft³ Low	(ASTM C-97) 150	—	117	—	—	135	—	—
Required Minimum	160	N.R.	110	135	161	140	150	160
High	190	—	—	—	185	—	—	170
WATER ABSORPTION (% By Weight ASTM C121) Low	(ASTM C-97) 0.02	—	(ASTM C-97) 3.6	0.6	2.8	(ASTM C-97) —	—	—
Required Maximum	0.40	NR	12	7.5	3	20	3	1
COMPRESSIVE STRENGTH (ksi) Required Minimum	(ASTM C-170) 19	NR	(ASTM C-170) 1.8	4.0	8.0	(ASTM C-170) 2	10	20
Maximum	52	35	—	12	32	—	—	37
MODULUS OF ELASTICITY (ksi × 10³) Low	2	—	0.6	—	—	1	—	—
High	10	—	—	—	1.4	—	—	7.5
MODULUS OF RUPTURE (ksi) Required Minimum	(ASTM C-99) 1.5	NR	(ASTM C-99) 0.4	0.5	1.0	(ASTM C-99) 0.3	1.0	2
High	5.5	—	—	1.6	2.9	—	—	—
ABRASION RESISTANCE (ASTM C-241)	NA	—	10	10	10	8	8	8

N.R. = No Requirement

Table 1.1 (Continued)

CHARACTERISTICS	MARBLE				SLATE	
					Building Stone	
	Calcite	Dolomite	Serpentine	Travertine (see Sec.1.3.1)	Exterior	Interior
GEOLOGY	Metamorphic			Sedimentary	Metamorphic	
MINEROLOGY	Calcite, Dolomite or Serpentine			Calcite, Dolomite	Quartz, Mica	
CHEMISTRY (approximate composition	$CaCO_3$ $MgCO_3$				$H_2Kal_3(SiO_4)_3$ $(H,K)_2(Mg,Fe)_2Al_2(SiO_4)_3$	
GEOGRAPHY	NY to AL, IN to MS, NE, KA, MO, OK, AR, TX, CO, SD, WY, CA, MN, WI				MA to GA, CA, AR	
COLORS	White, Gray, Red, Pink, Buff, Rose, Gold, Green, Yellow, Black, Brown, Tan				Blue, Green, Black, Purple Gray	
SIZE MAXIMUM ft² ASTM specification	20 C 503-79				— C 629-80	
DENSITY, lbs/ft³ Low	(ASTM C-97)					
Low	—	—	—	140	173	
Required Minimum	162	175	168	144	NR	
High	—	—	175	160	179	
WATER ABSORPTION (% By Weight ASTM C121) Low					(ASTM C-121)	
Low	0.65	—	0.10	—	0	0
Required Maximum	0.75	0.75	0.75	0.75	0.25	0.45
COMPRESSIVE STRENGTH (ksi)	(ASTM C-170)					
Required Minimum	7.5				N.R.	
Maximum	28.0				—	
MODULUS OF ELASTICITY (ksi × 10³) Low	2.0				—	
High	15.0				—	
MODULUS OF RUPTURE (ksi)	(ASTM C-99)				(ASTM C-120)	
Required Minimum	1.0				7.2 (Parallel to Grain)	
High	4.0				9.0 (Perpendicular)	
ABRASION RESISTANCE (ASTM C-241)	10				8	8

N.R. = No Requirement

Travertine marble has a Group D soundness classification. This highly colored and variegated stone is one of the most often specified marbles. Due to its relatively large proportion of faults and variety of working qualities, travertine requires extra care. Maximum size of units should be restricted or reinforcement employed. The 1985 Uniform Building Code lists travertine separately from marble.

The variegation of travertine is such that it has natural voids that should be filled. This prevents the undesirable penetration of water, dirt, and possibly even insects through the stone and into the structure. Travertine should be filled by a finisher in his shop, but if necessary, filling can be done at the job site.

The selection of filling materials should be left to the finisher, who knows what materials work best with his stones. Common materials used are natural gray or tinted Portland cement and clear or colored epoxy or polyester resins.

1.4 Thickness

Standard thicknesses for stone slab veneer are normally given metrically, these are 2 cm (¾''), 2.5 cm (⅞''), 3 cm (1¼''), 4 cm (1½'') and 5 cm (2''). The metric thicknesses are based on full centimeter measurements whereas the English equivalents are approximate. When stones thinner than 2 cm are specified, the strength, veining, size and thickness should also be considered. Typically stone veneers thicker than 5 cm, or 2'', are usually considered as cubic stock.

1.5 Sizes

Stone is a natural material with countless variations available. Particular stones will have various physical characteristics that may vary greatly.

It is usually not possible nor economically feasible to increase the strengths of the stones. Size, therefore, quite often becomes a limiting factor when selecting different stones.

Stones are usually quarried in blocks large enough to produce the fabricated sizes shown in Table 1.2. The sizes given in Table 1.2 may be considered standard maximum fabricated sizes. Larger sizes may be available for special cases.

Slabs larger than those typically fabricated may be subjected to handling and erection stresses that can cause damage or breakage. When stones larger than the standard maximum sizes are desired or required, special attention must be given during handling. Reinforcing the slabs with strengthening elements such as strong backs is sometimes required to ensure the stones' safe handling and erection. A strong back system reinforces the stone from the back by fastening a stiffener to the stone, as shown in Figure 1–1. This, in effect, reduces the stress within the stone by resisting the lateral loads.

1.6 Color and Veining

The color, veinings, clouds, mottlings and shadings in marble are caused by substances included in minor amounts during the rocks' formation. Iron oxides make the pinks, yellows, browns and reds. Most grays, blue-grays and blacks are of bituminous origin. Greens are caused by micas, chlorites and silicates.

Table 1.2 Typical Maximum Fabricated Sizes

CLASSIFICATION	TYPICAL MAXIMUM FABRICATED SIZES	
GRANITE	6'0'' wide × 8'0'' long	(182 cm × 244 cm), 48 sq. ft.
GROUP A MARBLE	5'0'' wide × 7'0'' long	(152 cm × 213 cm), 35 sq. ft.
GROUP B MARBLE	2'6'' to 5'0'' wide 4'0'' to 7'0'' long	(76 cm to 152 cm), (122 cm to 213 cm), 10–35 sq. ft.
GROUP C MARBLE	2'6'' to 4'0'' wide 4'0'' to 7'0'' long (Reinforcement employed when necessary) (Maximum 20 square feet [approximately 2 square meters] per piece recommended)	(76 cm to 122 cm), (122 cm to 213 cm)
GROUP D MARBLE	2'6'' to 4'0'' wide 4'0'' to 7'0'' long (Reinforcement employed when necessary) (Maximum 20 square feet [approximately 2 square meters] per piece recommended)	(76 cm to 122 cm), (122 cm to 213 cm)

NOTE: Using smaller stone sizes tends to speed up selection and delivery. Stone contractors and fabricators should be consulted before a final jointing scheme is selected.

Chapter 30 of the Uniform Building Code limits the size of individual pieces of thin stone veneer to 20 square feet or less in area. Engineered systems that are designed to resist calculated loads may exceed this limitation.

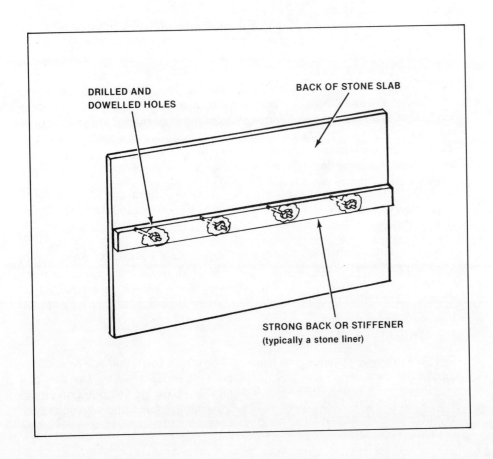

Figure 1–1
Strong back reinforcing system.

2
Selection of Building Stone

2.1 Exterior Applications

Successful applications of exterior veneer on various types of structures have made building stone a very recommendable and desirable solution to enclosure problems. The flexibility of the application of building stone has optimized the cost-effectiveness. This is especially true with the wide variety of architectural features, such as color, texture and pattern that can be achieved.

The choice of building stone for exterior application is made on the basis of three fundamental criteria: durability, color, and surface finish.

2.1.1 Durability

Durability is a characteristic of the material to withstand climatological effects, resist atmospheric agents, and attack from pollutants.

A distinction should be made between weathering and decay of stone. Not all changes by weathering agents are necessarily undesirable or harmful in that they do not always destroy or materially alter the natural integrity of the stone within a given length of time, although when exposed to the processes of weathering, all material must ultimately decompose or disintegrate. For example, some changes in color may not materially affect the integrity of the stone but may be desirable for architectural or aesthetic effects, giving an appearance of age. Hence, the element of time must enter into the evaluation of weathering in terms of modes and environmental conditions of use insofar as these can be evaluated satisfactorily.

2.1.2 Color

Color is a particularly important feature in architectural design. Selection of color can be aided by contacting the marble or stone contractors as the most reliable source of information. It is also suggested that a local contractor be contacted to determine the availability of certain colors and types of building stone in the area.

2.1.3 Surface Finishes

Stone surfaces can be finished in a number of ways, the smoother and more highly polished the finish is, the more apparent the color and veining will be. Rougher finishes on the other hand will cause the color and veining to be less obvious. Typical finishes are:

POLISHED FINISH—A reflective finish. Color and veining is maximized with this highly reflective finish.

HONED FINISH—There is little or no shine on this smooth finish.

SAND-FINISHED—A non-glossy dull surface; good for exterior applications.

ABRASIVE FINISH—A flat, non-reflective slightly roughened surface; excellent for exterior use.

FLAME FINISH—A plane, non-reflective surface with highlighted accents, usually recommended for external and paving use. The surface coarseness varies depending on the grain structure of the granite.

BUSH-HAMMERED—A corrugated finish, smoother on small surfaces, with interrupted parallel markings depending upon actual finishing: 8–cut (marking not over $\frac{3}{32}$'' apart), 6–cut (coarser with markings not over $\frac{1}{8}$'' apart, and 4–cut (coarsest, with markings not more than $\frac{7}{32}$'' apart).

The glossier and more highly reflective surfaces require more fabrication and finishing than the less finished surfaces, consequently the closer the stone gets to a polished surface the more expensive it is going to be. An abrasive finish is often the most economical for exterior use.

Other finishes, such as machine tooled, split or rock-faced, chat or shot sawn or tooled, are also available.

Table 2.1 lists the various typical finishes that can be obtained on different types of stone.

2.2 Interior Veneer

In interior veneer applications, the aesthetic factor is of significant importance; colored and veined marbles are usually used since they present many decorative features.

In the architectural application of stone veneer, there are many features that can be achieved, depending on the type of material. One of these features is the pattern of panel placement.

2.2.1 Veneer Patterns

Specific patterns or arrangements of the stone are possible only with the more highly veined stones such as certain marbles (see Figures 2–1 through 2–3).

The natural folds and veins found in marble create a distinctive marking trend throughout the stone block that is necessary for a pattern. Granite is generally too uniform in color and texture to achieve a specific pattern.

Formal patterns such as the slip pattern and end pattern (see Figures 2–1 through 2–3) require careful selection which of course increases the installed cost of the stone veneer.

Table 2.1 Building Stone Surface Finishes

GEOLOGICAL CATEGORY	COMMON NAME	FINISHES
1. SEDIMENTARY	Sandstone Limestone Dolomite	A) Smooth (machine finished by saw, grinder or planner) B) Machine tooled (with uniform grooves) C) Chat Sawn (non-uniform) D) Shot Sawn (irregular and uneven markings) E) Split Face (concave-convex) F) Rock Face (convex)
2. METAMORPHIC	Marble Serpentine Onyx Slate[1] Quartzite[1] Gneiss[2] Travertine[4]	A) Sanded B) Honed C) Polished D) Wheelabraded E) Bush-Hammered F) Split Face G) Rock Face
3. IGNEOUS	Granite Syenite Diorite[3] Gabbro Andesite Basalt	A) Sawn B) Honed C) Polished D) Machine Tooled (4-cut, 6-cut, chiseled, axed, pointed, etc.) E) Flamed F) Sand Finished G) Split Face H) Rock Face

[1] Slate and quartzite cannot be polished.

[2] Gneiss will take all of the finishes of marble and may also be flame finished.

[3] Diorite will not take flame finish.

[4] Travertine is actually a limestone but is classified with marbles for surface finishes. Travertine finishes include filled, partially filled, and unfilled.

Large blocks of stone are quarried for fabrication into thin stone slabs. It is a good practice to cut and finish the slabs so that they will be attached to the structure in the same plane they were in the quarry. This helps reduce potential problems, especially in freeze-thaw areas.

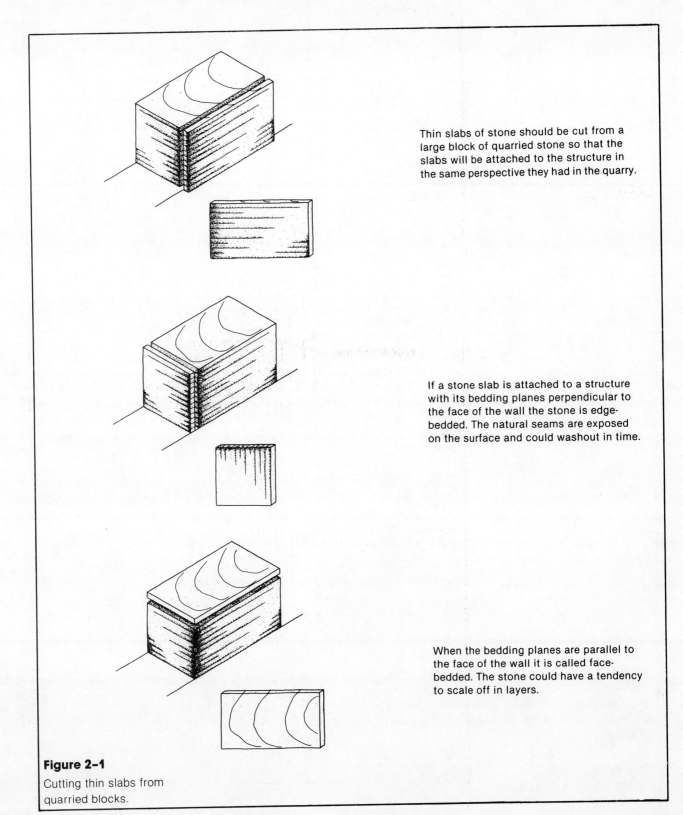

Thin slabs of stone should be cut from a large block of quarried stone so that the slabs will be attached to the structure in the same perspective they had in the quarry.

If a stone slab is attached to a structure with its bedding planes perpendicular to the face of the wall the stone is edge-bedded. The natural seams are exposed on the surface and could washout in time.

When the bedding planes are parallel to the face of the wall it is called face-bedded. The stone could have a tendency to scale off in layers.

Figure 2-1

Cutting thin slabs from quarried blocks.

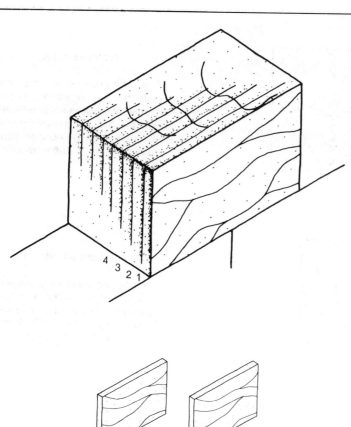

Quarried block of stone
ready for fabrication
into slabs.

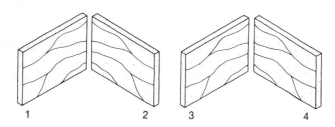

Finishing for blend or
slip patterns is on the
same face of each slab.

Finishing for matched
patterns is on adjacent
faces.

The drawings shown here in Figure 2–2 are
idealized, actual stone patterns will have slight
variations due to the portion of the stone that
will be lost during fabrication and sawing. For
optimum pattern uniformity panel arrangements
should be planned for groupings of four panels
of equal size.

Figure 2–2
Typical marble veining patterns.

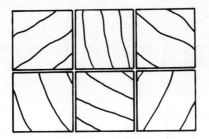

BLEND PATTERN

A random arrangement of stone panels that may or may not be from the same block arranged to uniformly blend the different stones into the wall. If no pattern is specified then a blend pattern will be provided.

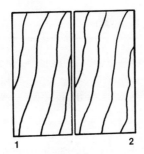

SLIP PATTERN

Stone slab panels are placed side by side so that veining patterns run parallel with each other: usually done with stones from the same block.

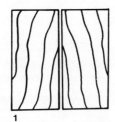

MATCH PATTERN

Stone panels from the same block are inverted and finished on adjacent faces so the veining will be a true mirror image.

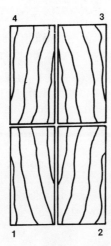

QUARTER or DIAMOND MATCHED PATTERN

A combination of book matching stone slab veneer from the same block so that veining patterns are mirror imaged in the adjacent stones.

3

Design Requirements

Stone slab veneer is a non-structural element applied to a backup supporting structure. Its use has existed for a long period of time and many methods have been developed for its installation and support.

Various building codes have listed some installation methods which have evolved from experience as standard practice rather than by an engineering procedure. The 1985 Uniform Building Code has provided that veneers may be designed based on engineering principles, but certain specification type installation methods may be used in lieu of engineered design.

3.1 Code Requriements

Chapter 30 of the 1985 Uniform Building Code lists certain general limitations for the design and construction of stone and marble. Important design requirements of veneer are:

- The design shall provide for differential movement of veneer and supports.

- Supporting structures to which veneer is attached shall be designed for the additional loads imposed by the veneer.

- Anchored stone slab veneer must be designed for a horizontal force of twice the weight of the veneer.

- Adhered veneer units cannot measure more than 36 inches in the greatest dimension nor more than 720 square inches in total area and shall weigh not more than 15 psf unless approved by the building official. Units weighing less than 3 psf are not limited in dimension or area.

- Anchored veneer shall be supported by non-combustible, corrosion-resistant structural framing having horizontal supports spaced not more than 25 feet above the adjacent ground elevation and not over 12 feet vertically above the 25 foot height (see Figure 3–1).

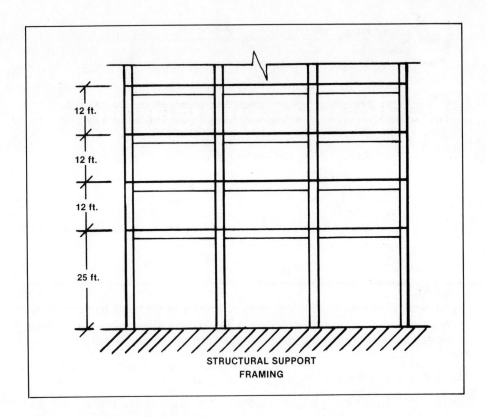

Figure 3–1
Maximum spacing of structural supports for anchored veneer.

3.2 Design Principles

If an engineering system of stone cladding is specified, an engineer should be consulted to determine the maximum expected deflection and movement of the structure. An engineered design will help select the most viable solution for the suspension system.

The design criteria established by the building code may be supplemented by additional requirements of the architect and/or engineer.

3.2.1 Design Criteria

For a properly designed and functional support system, the architect, engineer and stone contractor must consider all other factors that may affect the system.

3.2.1.1 Lateral Load

The lateral forces due to wind or seismic forces must be calculated so the anchoring system can be safely designed. The attachment system must be designed to resist a horizontal force equal to at least twice the weight of the veneer. A panel or framing system must be designed to resist twice the weight of the entire system, both the frame and stone.

> **Example:** What is the design lateral force for a 2'' marble slab subjected to a basic wind speed of 70 mph? Individual panels are up to 110' above the ground.

> **Solution:** From Table No. 23–F of the 1985 Uniform Building Code, the wind stagnation pressure (q_s) at standard height of 30' is 13 psf.

Calculating the equivalent static wind pressure where
$C_e = 1.3$, $C_q = 1.2$, $I = 1.0$
$p = C_e C_q q_s I = (1.3)(1.2)(13 \text{ psf})(1.0) = 20.3 \text{ psf}$

Section 3004(c) of the 1985 Uniform Building Code states that the veneer and its attachments must be designed to resist horizontal forces equal to twice the weight of the veneer.

From Table 1.1 the density of dolomite marble is found to be 175 pcf, therefore a 2'' marble slab weighs
$W_p = (175) 2''/12 = 29.2 \text{ psf}$.

Therefore since the weight of the slabs are greater than the wind loads, the lateral forces due to weight govern. The design lateral force $= 2 \times 29.2 = 58.4 \text{ psf}$.

3.2.1.2 Differential Movement

Special consideration should be given to all differential building movement. The structural lintels and horizontal supports must not allow deflections greater than 1/500 of the span under the full load of the veneer.

3.2.1.3 Thermal Movement

Different materials are going to have different rates of thermal expansion, therefore the maximum differences in thermal expansion must be considered in designing the veneer spacing support systems. In North America, temperature changes of stone veneer and structural supports can be as high as 170°F., depending on the color and texture. On very hot days, a masonry wall can have thermal expansion of up to one-half inch for a 100-foot-long wall. Thermal expansion of reinforced concrete is approximately the same as reinforced masonry. Expansion of insulated steel may be 0.6 of an inch for a 100-foot-long wall. Table 3.1 gives typical thermal expansion coefficients of various building materials.

3.2.1.4 Deformation

As a building is constructed, loads increase and elastic deformation occurs in heavily stressed elements. The designer should allow for this expected deformation in his details. Delaying application of veneer until late in construction or until after the majority of the dead load elements have been constructed will reduce these problems.

For long-term deformation (creep), additional clearances must be provided. Tall reinforced concrete frame buildings will experience average deformations due to creep of 0.0039 percent of their height; possibly as much as 0.065 percent. There is insufficient data to give a definite value to reinforced concrete masonry, but the values for reinforced concrete and reinforced concrete masonry should be comparable.

3.2.1.5 Shrinkage

When the backup structure is concrete or concrete masonry, there will be shrinkage of the supporting surfaces after initial placement. Again, the designer should allow for possible movement and/or delay application of the cladding until after the majority of the shrinkage has occurred. Two-thirds of the shrinkage takes place within the first three months, and approximately

Table 3.1 Thermal Expansion Coefficients of Various Building Materials.

MATERIAL	AVERAGE COEFFICIENT OF LINEAL THERMAL EXPANSION (in/°F) X 10⁻⁶	THERMAL EXPANSION, In. per 100 ft for 100°F temperature increase	
		To Closest .01"	To Closest $\frac{1}{16}$"
CLAY MASONRY			
Clay or shale brick	3.6	0.43	7/16
Fire clay brick or tile	2.5	0.30	5/16
Clay or shale tile	3.3	0.40	3/8
CONCRETE MASONRY			
Dense aggregate	5.2	0.62	5/8
Cinder aggregate	3.1	0.37	3/8
Expanded-shale aggregate	4.3	0.52	1/2
Expanded-slag aggregate	4.6	0.55	9/16
Pumice or cinder aggregate	4.1	0.49	1/2
STONE			
Granite	4.7	0.56	9/16
Limestone	4.4	0.53	1/2
Marble	7.3	0.88	7/8
Sandstone	6.0	0.72	3/4
CONCRETE			
Gravel aggregate	6.0	0.72	3/4
Lightweight, structural	4.5	0.54	9/16
METAL			
Aluminum	12.8	1.54	1 9/16
Bronze	10.1	1.21	1 3/16
Stainless steel	9.6	1.15	1 >1/8
Structural steel	6.7	0.80	13/16
WOOD, PARALLEL TO FIBER			
Fir	2.1	0.25	1/4
Maple	3.6	0.43	7/16
Oak	2.7	0.32	5/16
Pine	3.6	0.43	7/16
WOOD, PERPENDICULAR TO FIBER			
Fir	32.0	3.84	3 13/16
Maple	27.0	3.24	3 1/4
Oak	30.0	3.60	3 5/8
Pine	19.0	2.28	2 1/4
PLASTER			
Gypsum aggregate	7.6	0.91	15/16
Perlite aggregate	5.2	0.62	5/8
Vermiculite aggregate	5.9	0.71	11/16

From Brick Institute of America, Technical Note 18, *BIA, McLean, Va.*

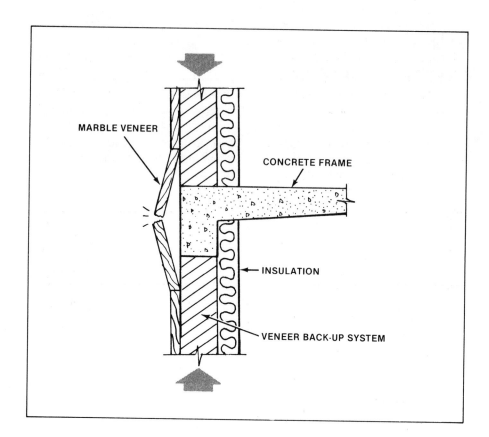

Figure 3-2

Veneer on building frame may buckle due to frame shortening if provision is not made for movement.

90 percent during the first year. When practical, start the stone installation after the poured-in-place concrete is completed. Due to cement hydration and loss of water, reinforced concrete walls shrink during the curing process as much as 0.00025 to 0.00045 times the length (see Figure 3-2).

3.2.1.6 Deviations

Variations from specified dimensions in the fabrication of the marble or stone or of the supporting structure require that the anchoring system be designed to allow that the final placement is in accordance with the plans and specifications. Slotted bolt holes and anchor bolts are typically used to allow for erection and fabrication tolerances (see Section 3.3.2).

3.2.1.7 Freeze/Thaw

Allowances must be made for the effects of freezing and thawing on stone cladding. Every cycle of freezing and thawing causes the internal moisture to expand and contract. This movement creates stresses in the veneer, the anchoring system and the supporting structure.

Stresses can be severe enough to move the veneer out of alignment, deteriorate anchor connections, and compromise the integrity of the veneer. The stone moves in relation to the anchor; the cladding moves in relation to the structure; the stone moves in relation to itself (stress damage, i.e., cracking), or any combination of these.

To reduce the possibility of freezing and thawing damage to the cladding, moisture must be controlled. Proper waterproof caulking (Sec. 3.6) of all joints will prevent water from entering from the outside. Waterproofing

(Sec. 6.2) the back of the marble and stone will prevent moisture from migrating through the stone. Proper flashing (Sec. 3.7) and weep holes (Sec. 3.8) will control the flow of any water that may collect behind the stone and direct this moisture to the outside of the cladding.

Example: Determine the required height of the horizontal joints for 1½''–thick marble veneer on a high-rise building attached to a concrete frame. Assume one-story height as shown below, for a building located in Seismic Zone 4. Individual marble slabs are 20 square feet each (4' high × 5' wide) and weigh 21 psf (168 pcf).

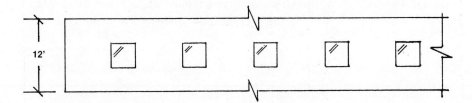

1. **Thermal Movement:** Assume 100°F. surface temperature differential. Reference Table 3.1.

    for concrete: 0.0000045(100°F)(12')(12''/1') = 0.065''

    for marble: 0.0000073(100°F)(12')(12''/1') = 0.105''

2. **Creep:** From Section 3.2.1.4., deformation due to creep for reinforced concrete averages 0.039 percent.

    0.00039 (12')(12''/1') = 0.056''

3. **Shrinkage:** From Section 3.2.1.5.

    0.00031 (12')(12''/1') = 0.045''

4. **Elastic Strain (deformation):** Approximation from Section 3.2.1.4

    0.00020 (12')(12''/1') = 0.029''

5. **Total Movement:**

    0.105 + 0.056 + 0.045 + 0.029 = 0.235''

    At least 0.235 inches of vertical space must be allowed in the 12'-high story height and maintained and detailed for in the design. Since sealants can only expand and contract approximately half their original size, twice the calculated size must be used.

6. **Joint Size:** Using typical 20 square foot stone panels (4' × 5'), the vertical floor span can be clad with

    12' ÷ 4' = 3 panels

    therefore the story has three joints. The size of the joints will be

    2(0.235'') ÷ 3 = 0.16'' each ∴
    use 3/16'' to 1/4'' joints

    Using typical ¼'' caulked waterproof joints between each stone slab will amply allow for the total expected movement of the story height.

7. **Check:**

    3 joints × 1/4'' each = 0.75'' actual
    > 0.47'' required ∴OK

3.3 Construction Tolerances

Natural stone and marble are used as thin cladding material in North America. It is therefore important to address the respective tolerances of the different materials when combining structural frames with stone veneer.

The allowable dimensional tolerances for structural frames are greater than commonly acceptable tolerances for stone veneers.

There are no code-approved allowable construction tolerances for thin stone veneers; however, the Construction Sciences Research Foundation specifies the recommended tolerances shown in Figure 3–3. Figure 3–3 depicts a comparison of allowable construction tolerances for the most common structural frames and also for industry-recommended stone tolerances. Current contract documents typically require that stone cladding be ''plumb and true to line'' and ''maintain flush face.'' This is more easily accomplished with the larger size pieces of stone than with the smaller pieces of unit masonry.

Due to the accepted allowable deviations in construction tolerances of steel and concrete, it is very difficult to set specific guidelines for stone veneers.

3.3.1 Design Considerations

When detailing thin stone veneer, the designer should allow for required and expected movements. This means using slotted holes for anchoring systems to allow for construction tolerances of the structural supporting frame. The supporting frame and joints between stone slabs must allow for differential movement, thermal movement, load-induced movement, and other considerations as previously mentioned in Section 3.2.

3.3.2 Architectural and Engineering Details

Stone veneer should not be expected to cover the mistakes of the structural frame materials. Exaggerated anchoring necessary to cover out-of-line framing could result in damage to both the cladding and the structure. Anchoring should provide sufficient adjustment to compensate for dimensional deviations which can be expected on the job. Each anchor should have provisions for variation in three directions for placement, as shown in Figure 3–4.

Section 2312(j)3.c of the 1985 Uniform Building Code states that ''nonbearing, non shear wall panels or similar elements'' such as stone slab veneer, ''which are attached to or enclose the exterior . . . shall accommodate movements of the structure resulting from lateral forces or temperature changes.''

''Connections and panel joints shall allow for a relative movement between stories of not less than two times story drift caused by wind or (3.0/K) times the calculated elastic story displacement caused by required seismic forces, or ½ inch, whichever is greater.''

Section 2312(h) of the 1985 Uniform Building Code states that the ''lateral deflections or drift of a story relative to its adjacent stories shall not exceed 0.005 times the story height unless it can be demonstrated that greater drift can be tolerated.''

Example: What is the required movement allowance for the connections and panel joints for a building with 12'-high stories?

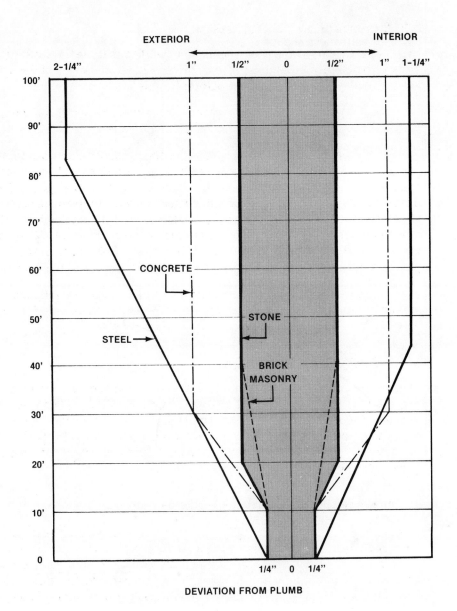

DEVIATION FROM PLUMB

Figure 3-3
Comparison of allowable
construction tolerances.

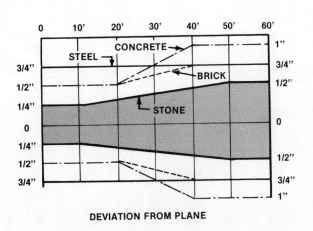

DEVIATION FROM PLANE

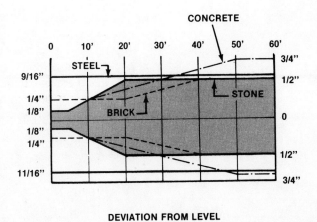

DEVIATION FROM LEVEL

22

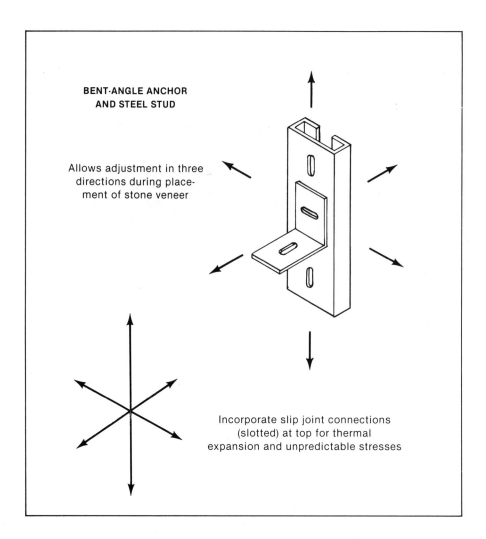

**BENT-ANGLE ANCHOR
AND STEEL STUD**

Allows adjustment in three
directions during place-
ment of stone veneer

Incorporate slip joint connections
(slotted) at top for thermal
expansion and unpredictable stresses

Figure 3-4
Typical bolted anchor detail
with slotted slip joint
connections.

First: Calculate maximum allowable drift between stories.

Drift = 0.005 (12') 12'' = 0.72''

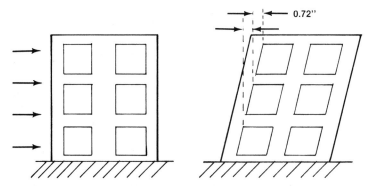

Second: Calculate allowable movement between stories. Use
maximum allowable drift between stories. Two times story
drift caused by wind:

2(0.72'') = 1.44''

or 3.0/K times the calculated elastic story displacement
caused by required seismic forces: K = 1, Z = ¾
(Seismic Zone 3)

3/k × Z × △ =

(3.0/1) (3/4) (0.72) = 1.62''

or ½, whichever is greater.

Use 1.62'' (1⅝'') = minimum design movement between stories

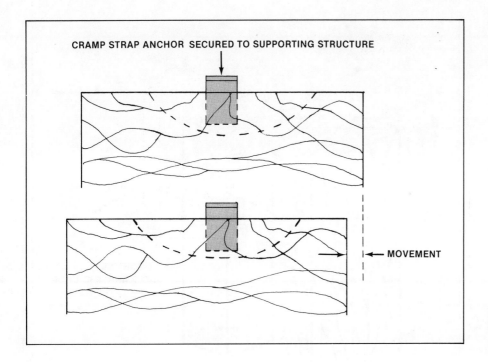

Figure 3–5
Cramp strap anchor.

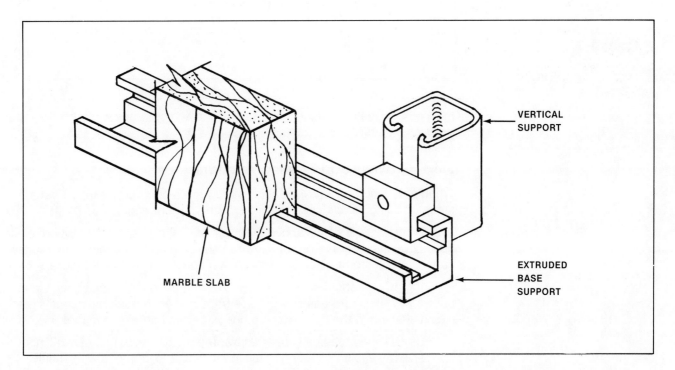

Figure 3–6
Extruded aluminum anchor.

Figure 3–5 gives an example of how this movement can be allowed for using a cramp strap anchor.

Another anchoring method would be continuous aluminum extrusions in continuous stone slots, as shown in Figure 3–6.

3.4 Loads

All stone cladding panels anchored to a building are subjected to gravity loads (the weight of the stone panel) and applied loads (wind or seismic). Anchors

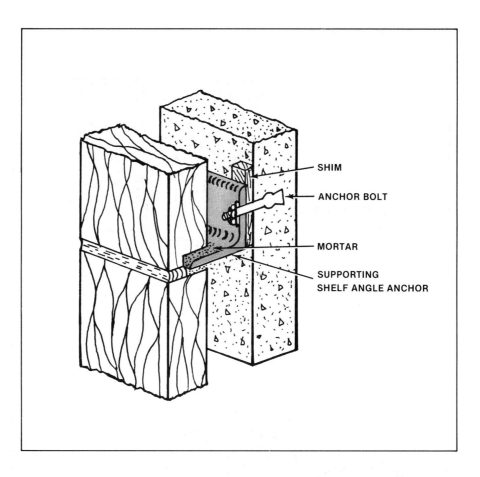

SHIM

ANCHOR BOLT

MORTAR

SUPPORTING
SHELF ANGLE ANCHOR

Figure 3–7
Supporting anchor, continuous
non-corrosive angle iron.

must be designed to safely support the stone against loads without inducing excessive stresses within the stone (see Figure 3–7).

3.4.1 Gravity Load-Bearing Anchors

When possible, load-bearing anchors are recommended to support natural stone cladding panels under or close to the bottom edge.

In the case of soffits above windows, or in similar conditions where exposed gravity anchors are not allowed under the bottom edge of the stone panels, it is customary to use epoxied and doweled liners (see Figure 3–8).

If gravity anchors cannot be applied under the bottom edge, then stone panels 2½''-thick or heavier can have bolts placed in non-continuous slots (key holes) cut in the back of the stone panels, as shown in Figure 3–9.

Stone veneer can be supported by properly designed mechanical, non-corrosive metal plug anchors drilled in the side and engaged with stainless steel or non-ferrous threaded rods supporting non-corrosive metal clip angles, as shown in Figure 3–10.

If plug anchors cannot be used (perhaps due to the sides being exposed), then another acceptable practice is the use of properly designed stainless steel or non-ferrous bent rods, set in polyester resin epoxy-fill or casting plaster, in back of the thin stone veneer (see Figure 3–11).

3.4.2 Lateral Loads

As per Section 3004 of the 1985 Uniform Building Code, all thin stone veneer ''shall be designed to resist positive and negative wind or seismic load forces

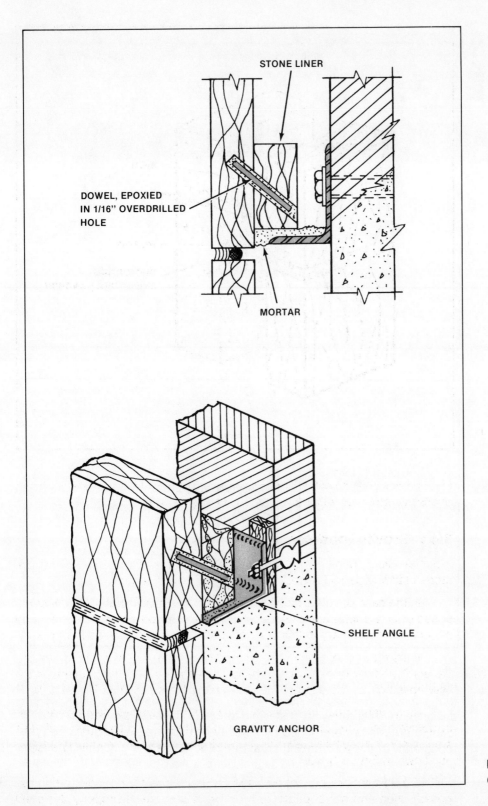

Figure 3–8
Gravity load-bearing anchor.

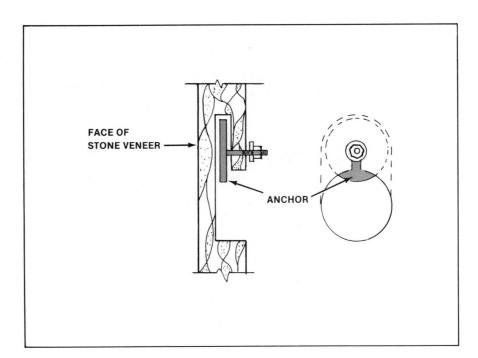

Figure 3-9
Keyhole anchor.

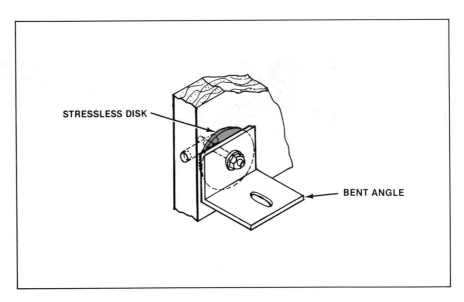

Figure 3-10
Metal plug anchor.

equal to twice the weight of the veneer.'' When a panel or framing system that supports multiple pieces of stone veneer is used, the supports are designed to resist the wind or seismic forces, whichever is greater. The wind loading criteria is determined by velocity of expected wind gusts and the topography of the surrounding area. For information and guidance in design of structures to resist wind and seismic loads, see Chapter 23 of the Uniform Building Code.

3.4.2.1 Wind Loads

As buildings become taller and individual stone slab veneer becomes larger in area, the lateral forces due to wind loads must be considered. Wind tunnel tests are often used on major structures to determine wind dynamics and force magnitude. Reinforcement is sometimes necessary for large, dimension slab veneer in critical areas.

3.4.2.2 Earthquake Loads

Thin stone and marble veneer must be designed and constructed to resist stresses produced by lateral earthquake forces. An anchoring system that does not conform to the applicable building code may be approved by the building official provided that evidence is submitted showing equivalent performance.

3.4.3 Lateral Load Anchors

Using lateral anchors in the joints between the cladding panels is recommended (see Figures 3–12 and 3–13). The number and distribution of the lateral anchors should be determined by calculations, good practice, and the requirements of the applicable building code.

Using multiple individual anchors is preferable to "split-tail" anchors.

When using "split-tail" anchors (Figure 3–14) or "drop-dowels" (Figure 3–15) to connect stone panels, it is recommended that the anchor or dowel cavity in the second stone panel be caulked with an elastic fast-curing silicone or low modulus polyurethane sealant.

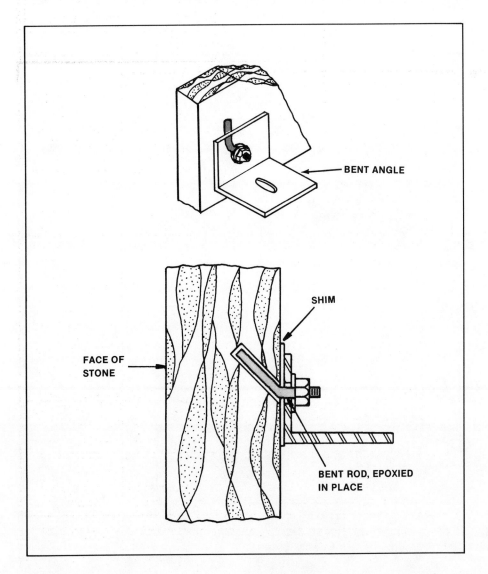

Figure 3–11
Bent rod anchor.

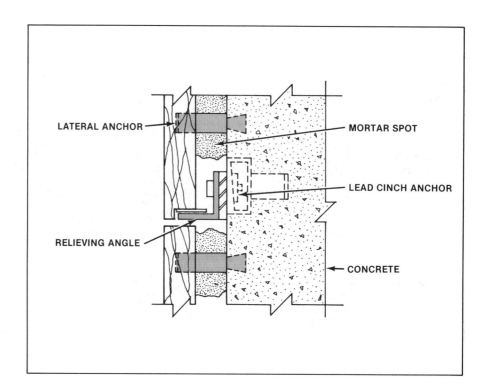

Figure 3–12

Lateral anchors and relieving angle.

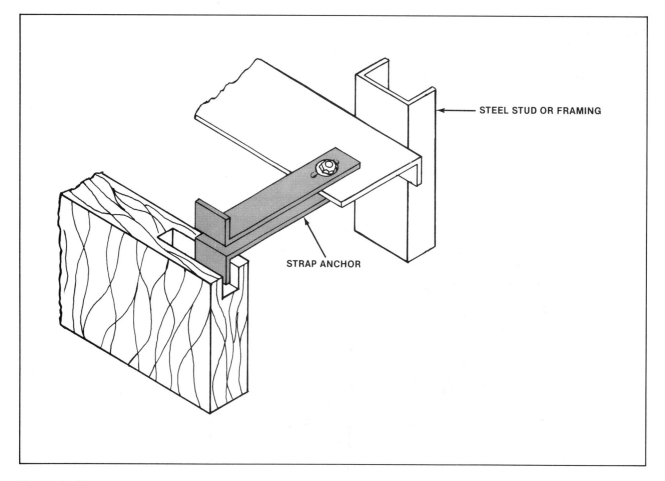

Figure 3–13

Strap anchors.

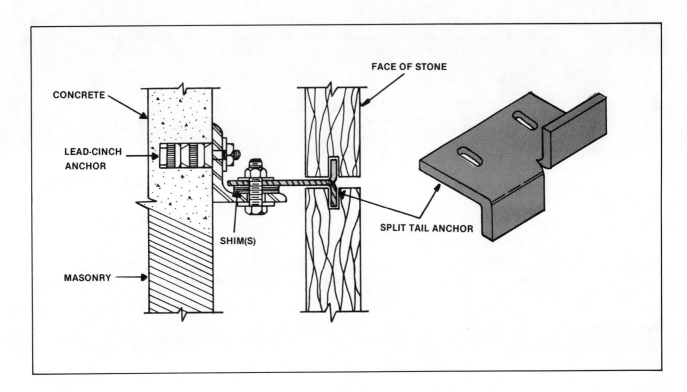

Figure 3–14

Split-tail anchor.

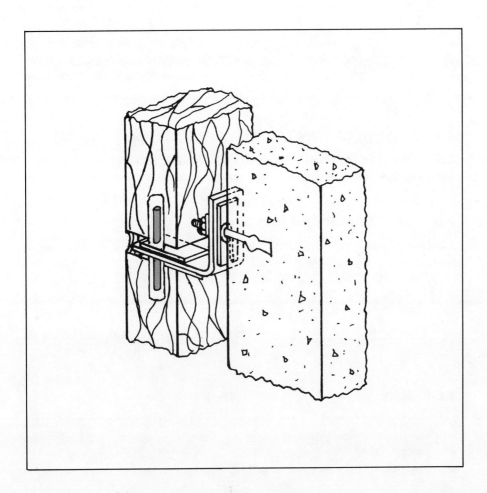

Figure 3–15

Drop-dowel anchor.

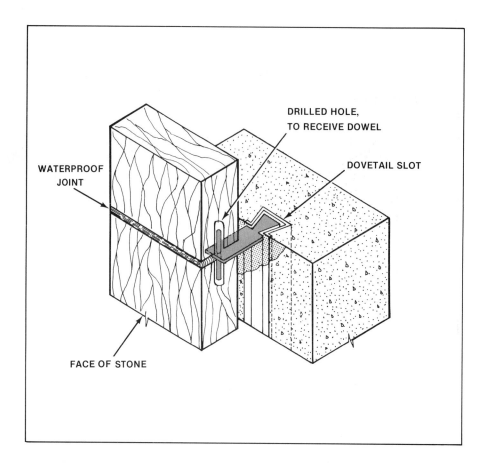

DRILLED HOLE,
TO RECEIVE DOWEL

DOVETAIL SLOT

WATERPROOF
JOINT

FACE OF STONE

Figure 3-16

Dovetail strap anchor with dowel.

The use of drilled holes on the edge of stone panels to hold dowels (Figure 3-16) is preferable to the use of slots (kerfs) to receive strap anchors (Figure 3-17). Stones of the same thickness, using round anchor holes, usually resist stresses better than stones with slots.

3.5 Selection of Gravity and Lateral Anchors

Supporting stone panels on the bottoms and sides is usually done with gravity anchors and lateral anchors.

3.5.1 Selection, Shape and Size

The shape, size and location of gravity and lateral anchors, as well as their attachment to the structure, must be carefully designed and calculated for all stresses to which they could be subjected, such as compression, tension, shear, bending and torsion. Gravity anchors can be attached on the top, bottom, sides or back of stone slab veneer.

Special attention is recommended in the design of horizontal joints under the gravity anchors to avoid any load transfer to the panel below.

3.5.2 Selection of Anchor Material

All metals in direct contact with stone must be non-corrosive and non-staining. The use of nylon shims to separate non-compatible metals from stone is a standard practice. Anchors not in direct contact with stone can be hot-dipped galvanized for exterior work or electro-galvanized or properly painted

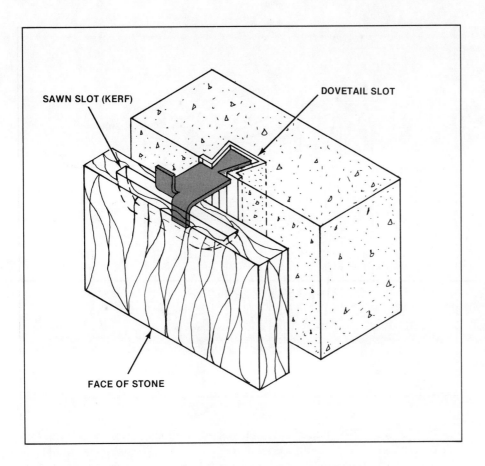

SAWN SLOT (KERF)

DOVETAIL SLOT

FACE OF STONE

Figure 3–17
Dovetail two-way strap anchor.

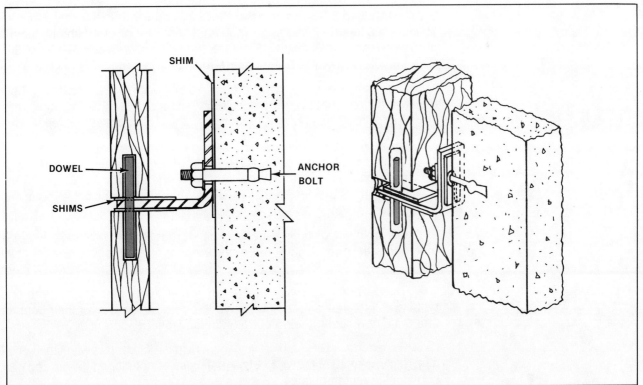

SHIM

DOWEL

SHIMS

ANCHOR BOLT

Figure 3–18
Dowel type gravity anchor.

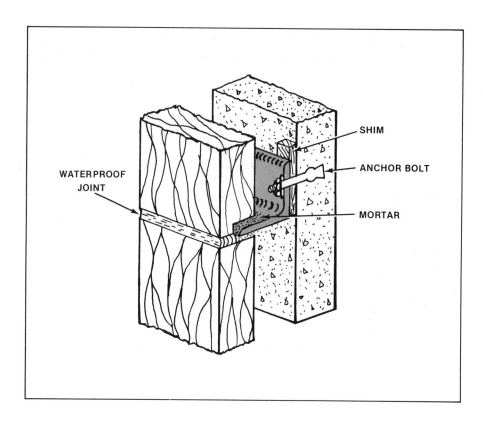

Figure 3-19

Gravity anchor.

for interior work. Hot-dipped zinc galvanized coatings can provide even better protection. Zinc coatings should have a corrosion resistance equal to or greater than 1.50 oz. per square foot of surface area for items less than $\frac{3}{16}$" in thickness and 2.00 oz. per square foot for items $\frac{3}{16}$" in thickness or over 15 inches in length. Items fully embedded in mortar or grout should have a corrosion resistance equal to or greater than 0.80 oz. per square foot of surface for wire and 0.60 oz. per square foot for sheet metal.

Care must be taken to avoid galvanic corrosion using non-compatible metals together without a proper isolator. In effect, the non-compatible metals will act similar to a battery, creating a voltage differential that reacts with and corrodes the less noble metal.

Galvanic corrosion occurs when a more noble metal such as zinc galvanizing comes in contact with a less noble metal such as copper in the presence of moisture. This will gradually deteriorate the less noble metal and impair the strength.

Galvanic corrosion is especially dangerous if the more noble metal is much greater in mass than the more susceptible less noble or sacrificial metal.

The degree of corrosion and deterioration will be determined by the ratio between the mass of the two dissimilar metals, the area of their contact and the difference in their electromagnetic (voltage) potential.

For exterior lateral and gravity anchors in direct contact with stone cladding, the use of 302-type or 304-type stainless or hot-dipped galvanized carbon steel is recommended.

Using anchors of Type 600 grade extruded aluminum is also standard trade practice. Aluminum wire, however, is not allowed as it does not have sufficient tensile strength.

Table 3.2 Recommended Metal-to-Metal Contacts						
METAL	ALUMINUM	CAST IRON	COPPER	GALVANIZED STEEL	PHOSPHOR BRONZE	STAINLESS STEEL
ALUMINUM	Y	N	N	N	N	N
CAST IRON	N	Y	N	Y	N	N
COPPER	N	N	Y	N	Y	cc
GALVANIZED STEEL	N	Y	N	Y	N	N
PHOSPHOR BRONZE	N	N	Y	N	Y	cc
STAINLESS STEEL	N	N	cc	N	cc	Y

Y = compatible—recommended
N = non-compatible—not allowed
cc = controlled condition; i.e. if presence of moisture is prevented, then use is permitted.

Electro-galvanizing, which is a very thin coating, does not provide reliable protection for exterior anchoring. Electro-galvanized anchors are liable to be scratched and thus are a potential source of corrosion.

Galvanized anchors in direct contact with limestone is not recommended. The electro-potential could cause electrolytic action when moisture is introduced and corrosion will occur.

Copper wire is widely used for interior natural stone installation and is corrosion-resistant.

Casting plaster of paris or gypsum plaster is unsuitable for use in exterior walls because they have little resistance to water penetration.

Table 3.2 gives recommendations for bi-metalic contacts for the most frequently used metals in natural stone construction.

3.6 Typical Joint Designs and Caulking

A factor in the design of successful building stone slab systems is the joints between stone panels. This detail is very important since it must prevent stresses and provide relief of the stresses due to movement of the stone or of the backup system (see Section 3.2 Design Principles). At the same time it must also furnish a weather-tight seal to prevent water leakage through the joints.

Joints can be divided into normal joints and expansion/contraction joints.

Normal joints are the ordinary joints between all the slabs, whereas expansion/contraction joints have the specific duty of absorbing the expansion and contraction movements of the structure of the building. A well-constructed normal joint is capable of partly covering the duties of an expansion joint so that the movement which it allows for can be sufficient to avoid

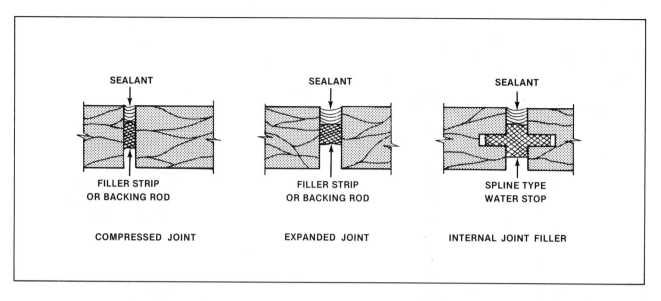

SEALANT
FILLER STRIP
OR BACKING ROD
COMPRESSED JOINT

SEALANT
FILLER STRIP
OR BACKING ROD
EXPANDED JOINT

SEALANT
SPLINE TYPE
WATER STOP
INTERNAL JOINT FILLER

Figure 3–20
Expansion and control joints.

compression in the veneered slabs. Normal joints should not be used in lieu of expansion/contraction joints.

When hydraulic mortar (i.e. Portland cement mortar) is used to seal joints, it should be placed as late as possible in the construction process and after the joints have been scraped clean and generously wetted.

3.6.1 Backing Rods

Modern construction practice uses backing rods placed in between the stone veneer units near the back or middle of the joint and then a caulking sealant is applied into the joint from the face side of the veneer. Refer to Figures 3–20 through 3–23.

An important feature in the determination of the joint sealant is the selection of the joint filler. The joint filler, or backing rod, performs three functions: it controls the depth of the caulking sealant; provides support for the caulking sealant when it is being compressed during tooling; and it acts as a bond breaker for the sealant to prevent three-sided adhesion. (Three-sided adhesion can result in failure of the sealant.)

Caulked waterproof joints are applied over joints that have backing rods inserted. The backing rods can be porous, called open celled, or non-porous, called closed cell, and are typically made of polyethylene or polystyrene rope.

3.6.2 Caulking

The best sealing is obtained with special caulking materials called sealants. These are typically highly plastic compounds, usually silicon or (poly) urethane. A good sealant should satisfy the following specifications:

- It must provide resistance, through time, to atmospheric agents without any marked alterations of its physical and chemical qualities;

- It must give constant adherence to the materials within which it is applied;

- It should be water-, air-, and dust-proof (impermiable);

- It should neither stain nor corrode the stone or adjacent material;

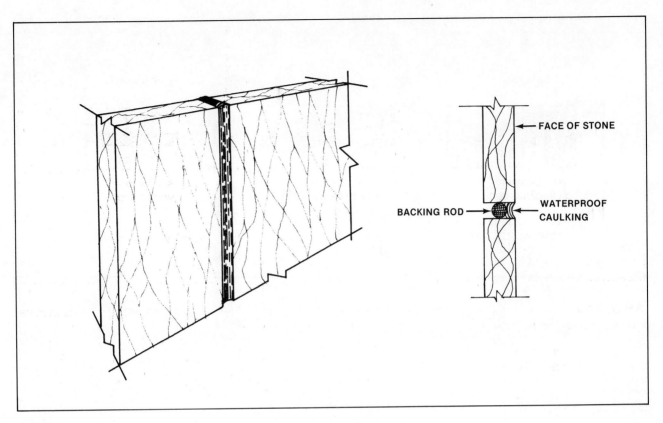

Figure 3–21
Flush wall joint.

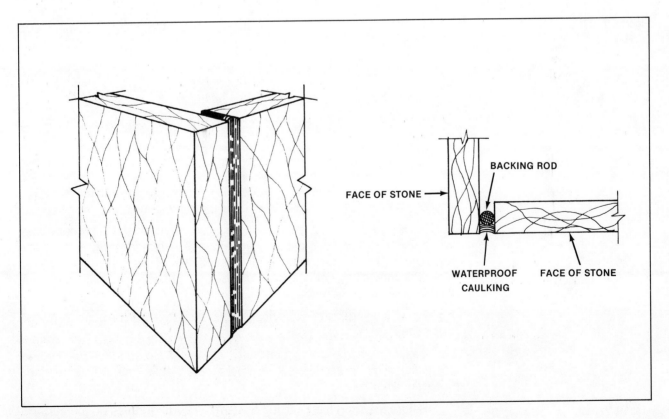

Figure 3–22
Butt joint.

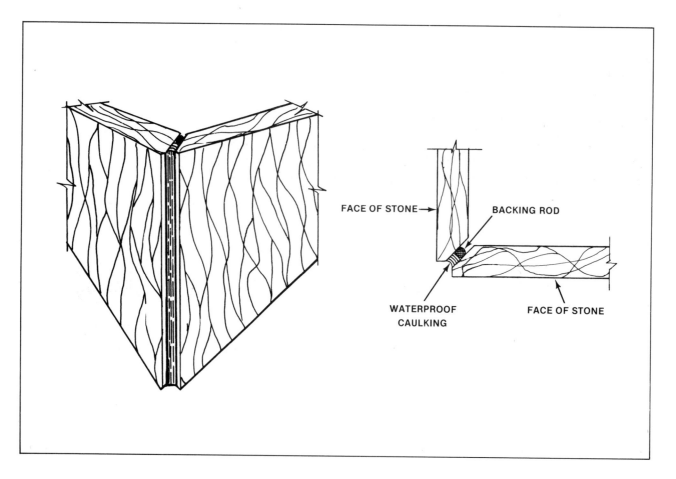

FACE OF STONE →

BACKING ROD

WATERPROOF
CAULKING

FACE OF STONE

Figure 3–23
Quirk joint.

- It should be plastic and not crack and should maintain its plasticity through time;
- It should not be affected by chemical agents which would normally be found in buildings, *i.e.*, mortar and cement alkalinity, maintenance substances, etc.;
- It should be compatible with other fillers used in the same joint.

The depth of the caulking material in the joint should be between ⅛'' and ⅜'' deep, or approximately half the joint width. Caulked joints in stone veneer are usually smaller than those found in regular brick masonry. Typical joints are ¼'' wide, and in some cases such as interior stone veneer, only ⅛'' wide. No caulked joint should be deeper than the joint width.

Particular care must be taken to ensure clean joints for proper adhesion. Sealant application must be in accordance with manufacturers' recommendations and before expiration of shelf life of the sealant. If stone thickness and setting conditions allow, sealing the back and front of the joint (double sealing) is recommended.

For critical areas, to avoid possible smears, tape can be used along the joint edges.

Gaskets, when used as joint fillers, are usually extruded or pre-formed for joints; slight pressure will compress the gasket for efficient water protection.

Before applying the caulking sealant, all kerfs or holes on the surface of the stone to which the sealant will be applied must be filled with a high-quality non-staining compatible sealant.

The caulking or sealing of stone veneer is one of the final steps in cladding construction. It is important to ensure that the sealing compound used is compatible with all other units and will perform correctly. These joints are to prevent moisture penetration and avoid the development of high stress from any movement of the marble or stone veneer or the supporting structure.

3.6.3 Mortar and Sealing Joints

To maintain the aesthetic appeal of marble and granite veneer, it is important to prevent the formation of stains on exterior veneered stone. It is necessary to ensure that the cement used in the mortar does not contain noxious

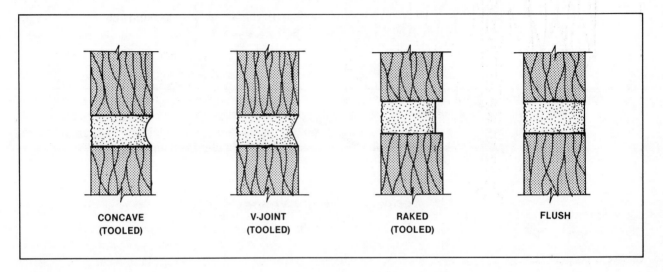

| CONCAVE (TOOLED) | V-JOINT (TOOLED) | RAKED (TOOLED) | FLUSH |

Figure 3–24
Typical Portland cement mortared joints.

components, such as blast furnace cements or a **high alkaline** Portland cement. Also, the aggregate should be carefully washed and free of clay, iron oxide and salt.

The compressive strength of the mortar used for joint sealing must be less than the compressive strength of the marble. This ensures that the mortar will fail first, thus allowing time to correct and repair the cause of the failure before the marble can be damaged or possible personal injury occur.

Typical Portland cement mortared joints are illustrated in Figure 3–24.

3.6.4 Epoxy Fill

Since the advent of thinner building stone, it has been observed that water will penetrate the thin stone veneer more readily than normally expected. Areas with the dark, damp appearance of moisture may occur on the face of the thin stone. This darker area is the result of moisture in the stone. The moisture flows through the natural faults and voids in the stone at different rates, blocked off in some areas, flowing readily through others, and evaporates as it reaches the face of the stone. The problem can be aggravated by kerfs in the edge of the stone.

Lining kerfs with an epoxy or polyurethane or applying a hydrophobic sealer or the use of a material that can prevent water being transmitted from the kerf edge to the face of the stone can be effective in eliminating the damp appearance problem.

The visual effect of lining and sealing material on the behaviour of the entire veneer should be evaluated prior to its use.

3.7 Flashing

There will be some water finding its way behind the stone cladding. Conden-sation also produces moisture, therefore water must be permitted to drain out from the setting space behind the stone by using properly designed weep holes and flashing.

Flashing can be a flexible material installed between the stone panel and the structure, one end higher up against the structure and turned at the other lower end into the stone joint, as shown in Figure 3–25. Commonly used flashing materials are waterproof, rubberized fabric, polyethylene or soft ne-oprene sheets or soft, thin guage stainless steel or copper flashings.

Flashing should be placed over all openings, lintels and continuous sup-port angles and ¼'' weep holes spaced every two feet along the flashing.

3.7.1 Copings

Moisture must be prevented from entering the wall from the top of the stone wall. Many designers use copings for this purpose and to enhance the appeal of their structures. A coping is usually a stone slab laid over the entire lateral edge of a wall and designed to prevent water from entering (see Figures 3–26 and 3–27).

3.8 Venting of Cavity Veneer Walls

Many veneer failures are the result of the improper venting of wall cavities. This is especially important where freezing and thawing can occur. Ventilating the air cavity behind the veneer allows water vapor that may enter the cavity behind the veneer to escape to the outside before freezing can take place.

Figure 3–25
Continuous waterproof flashing (typical detail for con-crete or masonry backup).

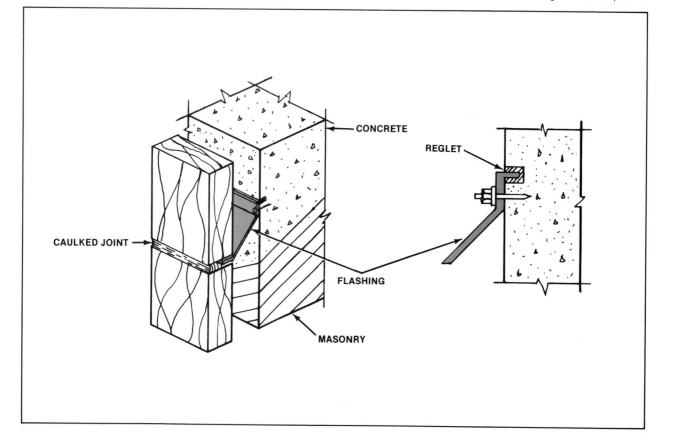

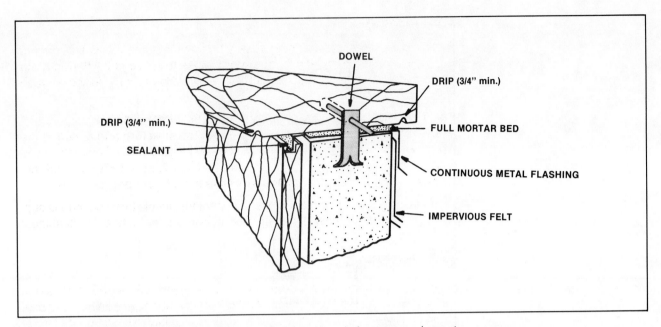

Figure 3–26
Molded marble coping (typical detail for concrete or masonry backup).

If water is trapped behind the veneer, it will expand as it freezes and exert pressure between the veneer and the structure that may cause the failure of the system. Figure 3–28 shows a typical cavity venting weep hole detail often used at intersections of horizontal and vertical joints.

The installation of stone slab veneer has evolved through the years. Previous standards developed from past experience when joints between stones were filled with a portland cement mortar and the building's interior was not climate controlled. Thus, the chances for condensation developing on the veneer was negligible.

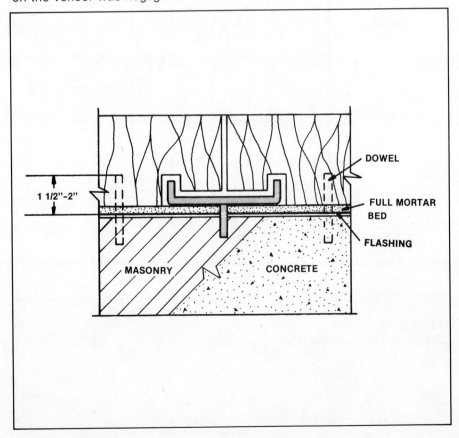

Figure 3–27
Coping anchor.

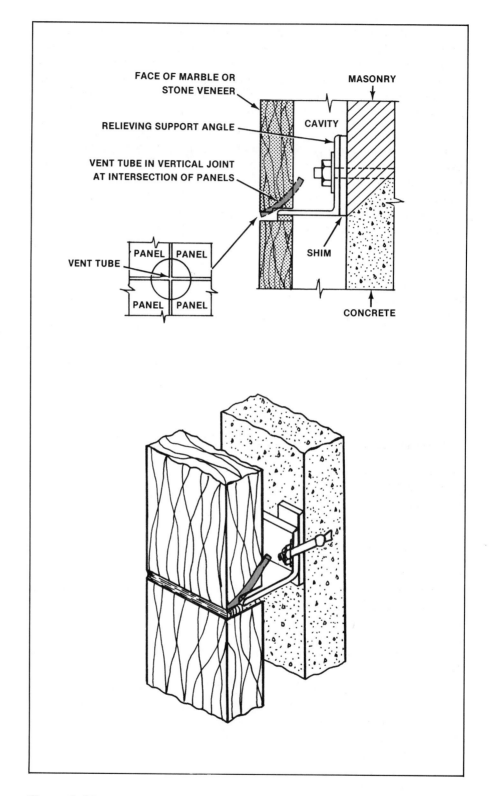

Figure 3-28
Cavity venting weep hole (detail).

Modern construction, however, is capable of producing structures that are nearly air tight. With joints sealed with vapor tight sealants and the building's interior climate controlled for temperature and humidity, the potential for condensation is much greater. Therefore, providing ventilation between the cavity and the outside environment is very important to help prevent moisture problems which can lead to failures in the sealant or anchor cladding.

If the cavity between the stone veneer and the structure was solid grouted, then wind-driven rain would be forced through the stone veneer and water would move from exterior to interior and vice versa, depending on the temperature and humidity differentials from outside to inside. If a waterproof barrier is applied to the exterior face of a supporting back-up wall without ventilating the veneer to the exterior environment then any moisture penetrating through the stone will have no exit or means of elimination from the building. The veneer may possibly crack or even separate from the back-up wall.

To prevent the potential for freeze thaw damage to the stones or anchors, it is best to leave an air space between the stone and the supporting back-up structure and vent this cavity to the outside air. The waterproof barrier is applied to the supporting structural back up and not to the stone, this insures equal air pressure on both sides of the stone and helps prevent condensation from developing. Also, if any water should penetrate through the stone or the joints it would be stopped at the cavity and drained back to the outside of the structure via properly designed flashing and weep holes.

Weep holes should be spaced every 2 feet along supporting angles.

3.9 Fabrication of Stone Panels

Fabrication must be in accordance with specifications and with approved shop drawings. Cutouts for other trades, if possible, should be provided in the shop. Tolerances should be within industry standards. Table 3.3 and Table 3.4 show allowable fabrication tolerances for marble and stone veneer.

3.9.1 Inspection

For larger projects, and when feasible, the stone slabs should be inspected in the fabricating plant for structural defects, acceptable color range, proper finish, and acceptable markings such as veining, seams, intrusions, etc. Such inspection will protect all parties—the fabricator, the stone contractor, the architect, and the general contractor—from disputes and will avoid the costly replacement of any rejected panels shipped to the job or installed on the building.

For composite panels, such as precast reinforced concrete with anchored natural stone or stone slabs pre-assembled on steel frames or trusses, inspection of the assembly is recommended to ensure that specifications and design details are followed. In many cases, the anchors, shelf angles, reinforcing steel, insulation and other components are not exposed to view. The consequences of improper assembly may not become evident until years after the panel is erected.

3.9.2 Handling

To prevent bowing, chipping and other damage, special care must be taken in handling and storing. The larger the stone, the greater the possibility of damage. As mentioned in Section 1.5, Sizes, using a stiffener on large stones will help prevent damage.

Stone slabs should be stored on "A" frames or special support frames so that the slab rests on edge.

Table 3.3   Allowable Fabrication Tolerances for Granite Veneer

FINISH/USE	LENGTH AND HEIGHT	CRITICAL DEPTH UP TO 1½" THICKNESS	CRITICAL DEPTH ABOVE 1½" THICKNESS	DEVIATION* FROM FLAT SURFACE EXPOSED FACE (4' span)	DEVIATION FROM SQUARE DIAGONAL
POLISHED	$\pm \frac{1}{16}$"	$-\frac{1}{16}$" $+\frac{1}{8}$"	$\pm \frac{1}{4}$"	$\pm \frac{3}{64}$"	$\pm \frac{1}{16}$"
RUBBED OR FINE SANDBLASTING		$\pm \frac{3}{8}$" (23")		$\pm \frac{3}{64}$"	
HONED OR FINE RUBBED	$\pm \frac{1}{16}$"	$-\frac{1}{16}$" $+\frac{1}{8}$"	$\pm \frac{1}{4}$"	$\pm \frac{3}{64}$"	$\pm \frac{1}{16}$"
SHOT GROUND		$\pm \frac{3}{8}$" (23")		$\pm \frac{3}{32}$"	
SAWN FINISH	$\pm \frac{1}{16}$"	$\pm \frac{3}{8}$" (23")	$\pm \frac{1}{4}$"	$\pm \frac{1}{8}$"	$\pm \frac{1}{16}$"
FLAMED		$-\frac{1}{16}$" $+\frac{1}{8}$"		$\pm \frac{3}{16}$"	

*Deviation between parallel edges of stone veneer should not exceed $\pm \frac{1}{16}$" per 4' span for in-yard setting or $\pm \frac{3}{32}$" for on-site setting.

Variations on polished, honed and fine rubbed surfaces at the bed and joint arris lines shall not exceed $\frac{3}{64}$" or $\frac{1}{8}$ of the specified joint width, whichever is greater.

On surfaces having other finishes, the maximum variation from true plane shall not exceed $\frac{1}{4}$ of the specified joint width.

Table 3.4   Allowable Fabrication Tolerances for Marble Veneer

	LENGTH AND HEIGHT	CRITICAL DEPTH UP TO 2¼" THICKNESS	CRITICAL DEPTH ABOVE 2¼" THICKNESS	DEVIATION* FROM FLAT SURFACE EXPOSED FACE	DEVIATIONS FROM SQUARE DIAGONAL
Polished Finish	$\pm \frac{1}{16}$"	$-\frac{1}{16}$" $+\frac{1}{8}$"	$-\frac{1}{8}$" $+\frac{3}{16}$"	$\pm \frac{1}{32}$"	$\pm \frac{1}{16}$"
Honed Finish	$\pm \frac{1}{16}$"	$-\frac{1}{16}$" $+\frac{1}{8}$"	$-\frac{1}{8}$" $+\frac{3}{16}$"	$\pm \frac{1}{32}$"	$\pm \frac{1}{16}$"

*Deviation between parallel edges of stone veneer should not exceed $\pm \frac{1}{16}$" per 4' span for in-yard setting, or $\pm \frac{3}{32}$" for on-site setting.

Variations on polished, honed and fine rubbed surfaces at the bed and joint arris lines shall not exceed $\frac{3}{64}$" or $\frac{1}{8}$ of the specified joint width, whichever is greater.

On surfaces having other finishes, the maximum variation from true plane shall not exceed $\frac{1}{4}$ of the specified joint width.

4

Installation and Anchor Details

Careful detailing of the anchoring system is very important. By considering all the different stone slabs and how they are going to operate as a unit, the designer can create an appealing and lasting structure.

When developing anchor details, the requirements as outlined in this chapter and in Section 3006 of the Uniform Building Code, Chapter 30, must be met. All anchor ties must be made of non-ferrous or stainless steel corrosion-resistant metal. Aluminum wire is not acceptable. All wire anchors must be fully embedded in Portland cement spots. Gypsum casting plaster can be used for interior installations (refer to Figure 4–1 through 4–3).

4.1 Anchoring

Slab stone veneer can be anchored in numerous fashions. Stone veneer can be mechanically installed to backup masonry or concrete with cement mortar or casting plaster around the anchors, as shown in Figures 4–4 through 4–6.

Veneer can also be mechanically installed directly to the building frame without using backup mortar or plaster (see Figures 4–7 and 4–8).

Stone panels can be mechanically anchored to a grid system or to a strut system, as shown in Figure 4–9.

As Figure 4–10 illustrates, thin slab stone veneer can also be installed using woven wire mesh and paper backup on steel frames or wood studs.

Figures 4–11 through 4–19 illustrate various methods of anchoring stone veneer. Table 4.1 shows strengths of standard veneer anchors in stone.

4.2 Anchoring Interior Veneer

The "spot and tie" method is usually the preferred method used to install interior stone slab veneer. The spot and tie method employs non-corrosive wire anchors of brass or copper spaced two feet on centers in accordance with the Uniform Building Code, or 18 inches on centers in accordance with the California State Building Code, around the perimeter of the individual stone slabs. One end of the wire anchor is grouted into a hole drilled in the edge of the stone and the other end is bent and inserted into an inverted bell-shaped hole in the backup wall. To ensure permanent anchorage and alignment, plaster of paris is used to encase the anchor wires and at intermittent spots between the back of the slab and the backup wall (see Figures 4–20 through 4–23).

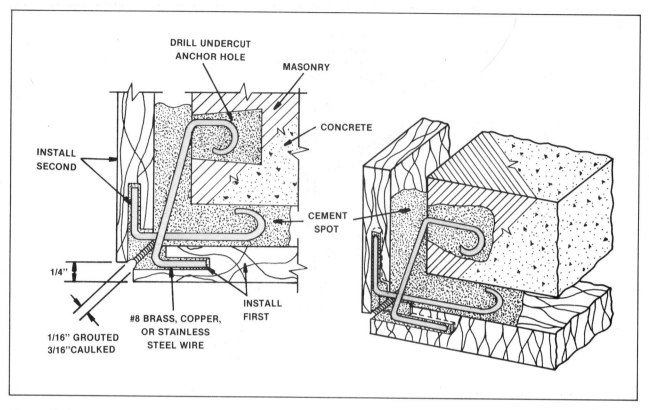

Figure 4–1
Quirk joint corner.

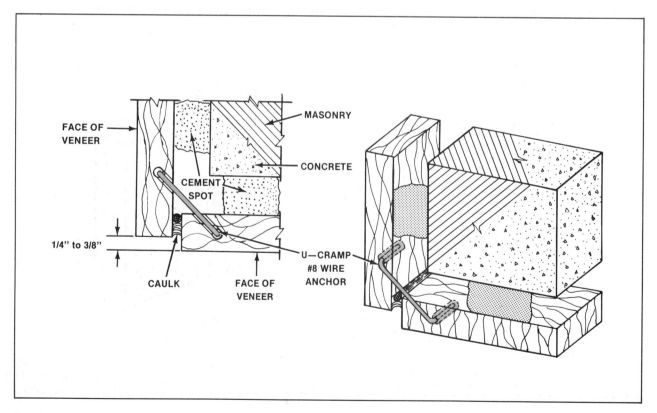

Figure 4–2
Corner detail.

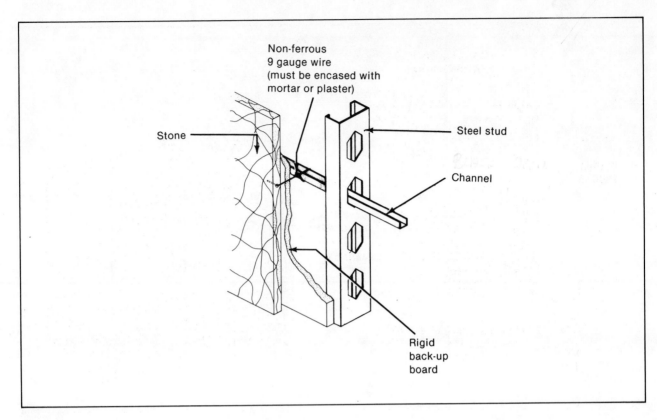

Figure 4–3

Stone veneer on steel studs.

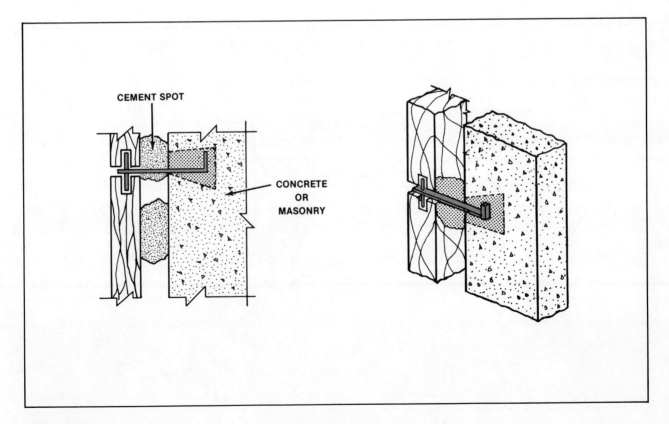

Figure 4–4

L-strap anchor with dowel.

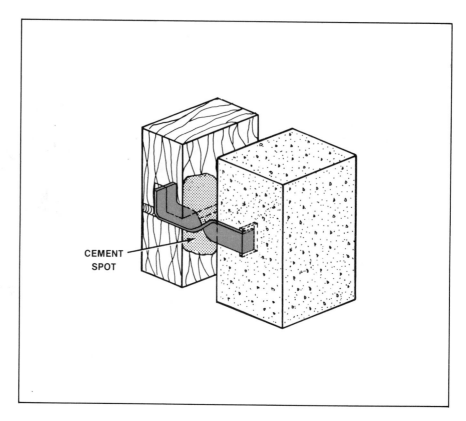

Figure 4–5
Twisted strap anchor.

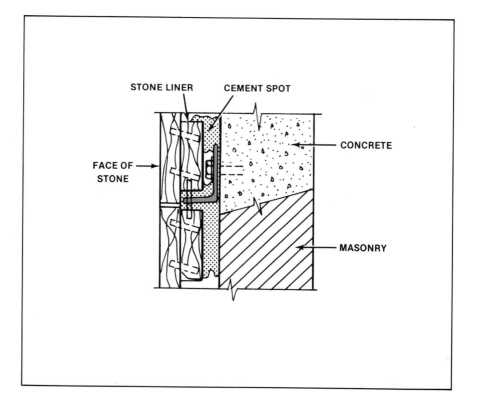

Figure 4–6
L-strap anchor with dowel and liners.

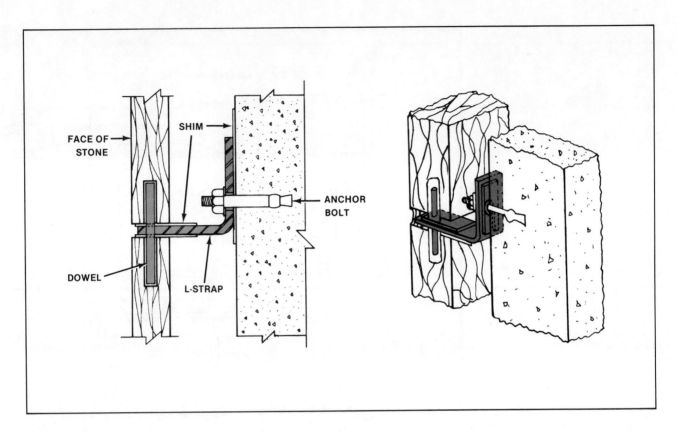

Figure 4-7
L-strap anchor with dowel.

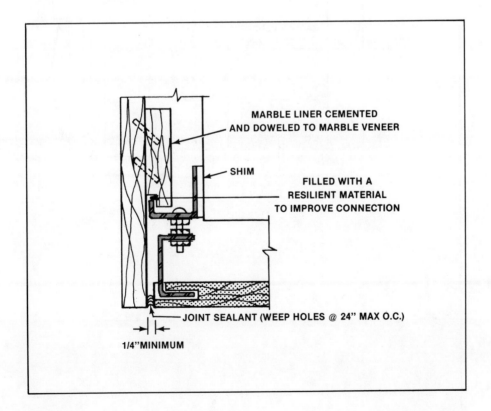

Figure 4-8
Soffit edge type hanger.

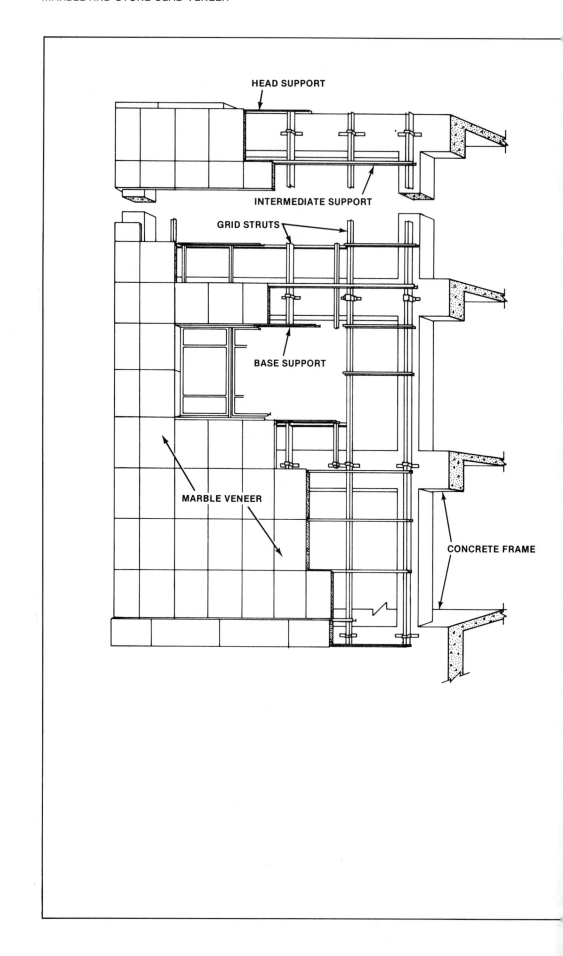

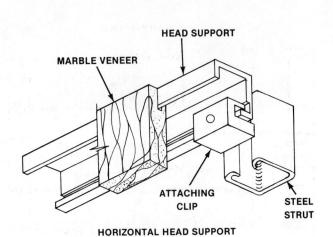

HORIZONTAL HEAD SUPPORT

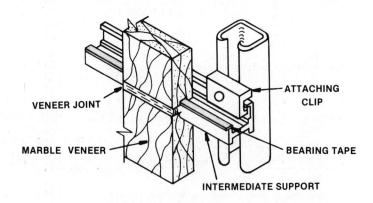

HORIZONTAL INTERMEDIATE SUPPORT

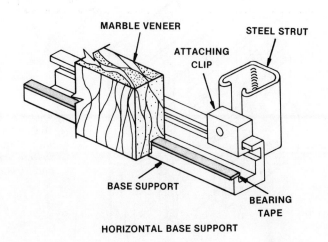

HORIZONTAL BASE SUPPORT

Figure 4-9
Mechanical grid mounted system.

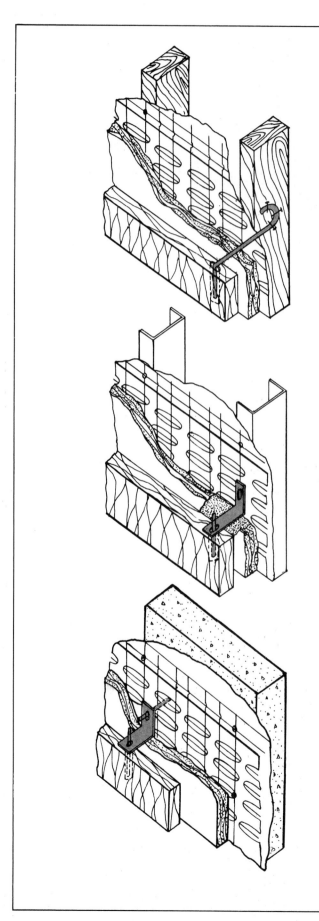

Anchored Stone Veneer
on Wood Studs with
wire reinforced lathing
system using #9 gauge
copper wire anchor.

Anchored Stone Veneer
on Steel Studs with
wire reinforced lathing
system using Metal Strap
and Dowel Anchor and
grout spot.

Anchored Stone Veneer
on Concrete with
wire reinforced lathing
system using Steel Strap
and Dowel system.

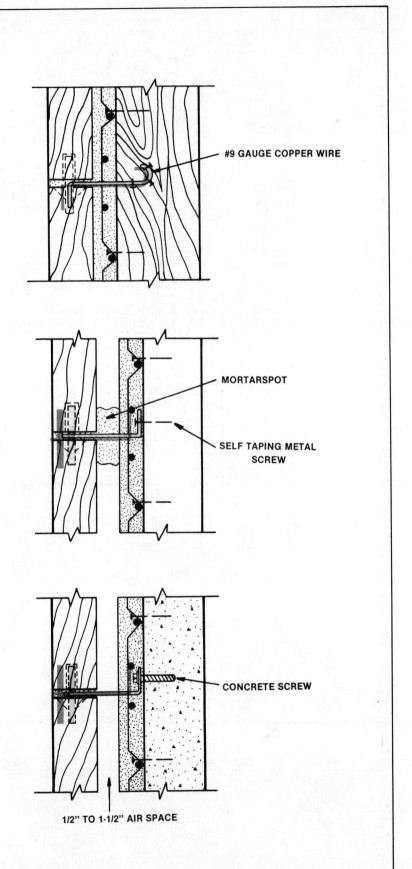

#9 GAUGE COPPER WIRE

MORTARSPOT

SELF TAPING METAL
SCREW

CONCRETE SCREW

1/2" TO 1-1/2" AIR SPACE

Figure 4–10
Anchoring veneer to cement
plaster.

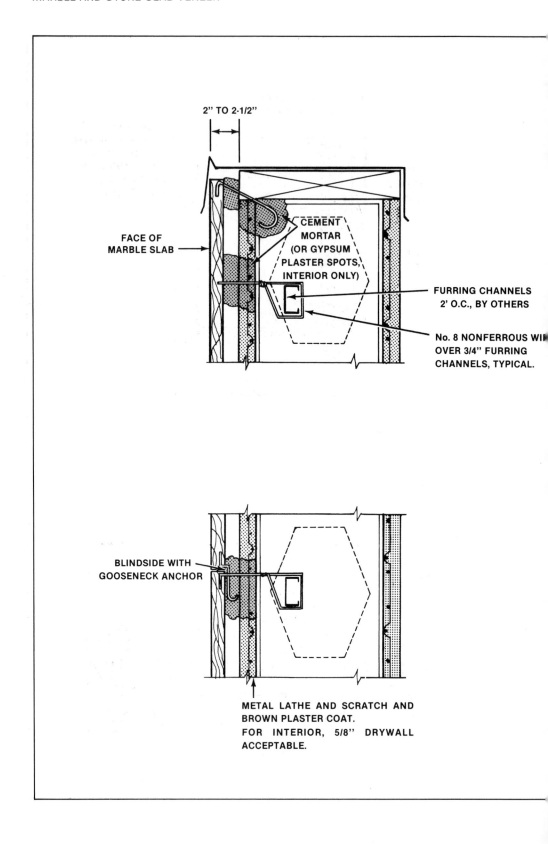

2" TO 2-1/2"

FACE OF
MARBLE SLAB

CEMENT
MORTAR
(OR GYPSUM
PLASTER SPOTS,
INTERIOR ONLY)

FURRING CHANNELS
2' O.C., BY OTHERS

No. 8 NONFERROUS WIRE
OVER 3/4" FURRING
CHANNELS, TYPICAL.

BLINDSIDE WITH
GOOSENECK ANCHOR

METAL LATHE AND SCRATCH AND
BROWN PLASTER COAT.
FOR INTERIOR, 5/8" DRYWALL
ACCEPTABLE.

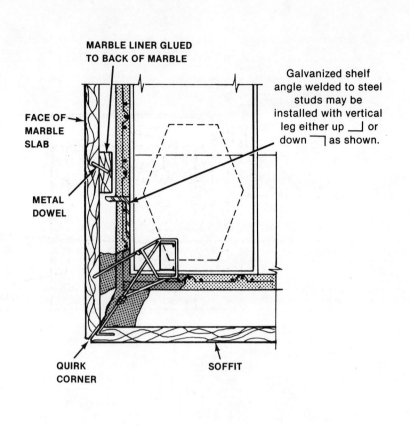

MARBLE LINER GLUED
TO BACK OF MARBLE

Galvanized shelf
angle welded to steel
studs may be
installed with vertical
leg either up ⌐ or
down ⌐ as shown.

FACE OF
MARBLE
SLAB

METAL
DOWEL

QUIRK
CORNER

SOFFIT

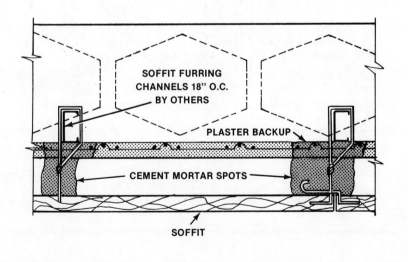

SOFFIT FURRING
CHANNELS 18" O.C.
BY OTHERS

PLASTER BACKUP

CEMENT MORTAR SPOTS

SOFFIT

Figure 4-11
Attachment of marble veneer
to metal stud and plaster walls
and soffits.

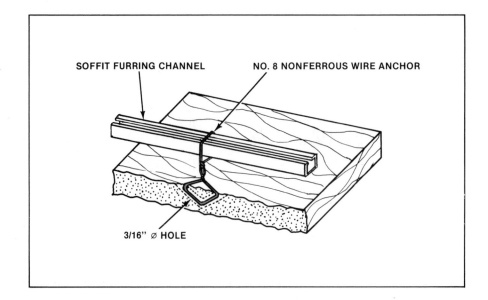

Figure 4–12
Intermediate lace tie anchor
for overhead installation.

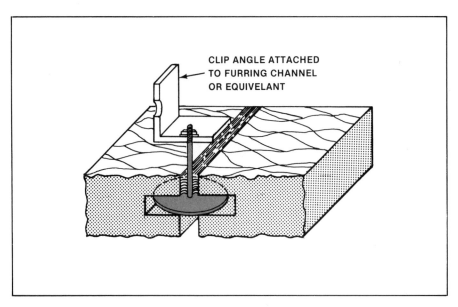

Figure 4–13
Disk soffit anchor.

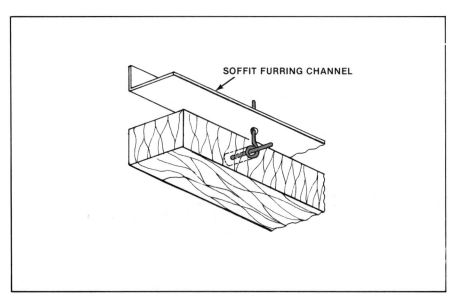

Figure 4–14
Eye rod and dowel soffit
anchor.

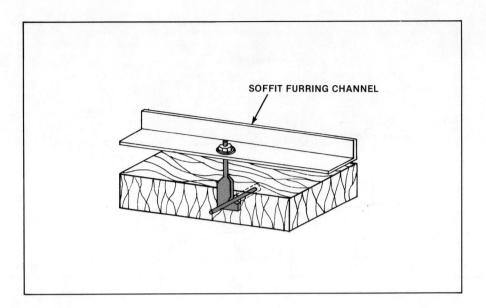

Figure 4–15
Bar strap with dowel soffit anchor.

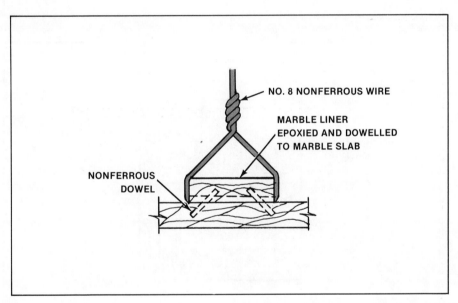

Figure 4–16
Wire soffit anchor and liner.

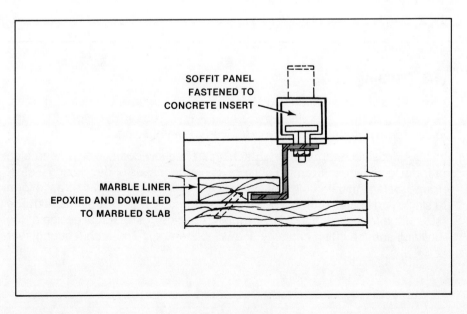

Figure 4–17
Soffit panel with marble liner.

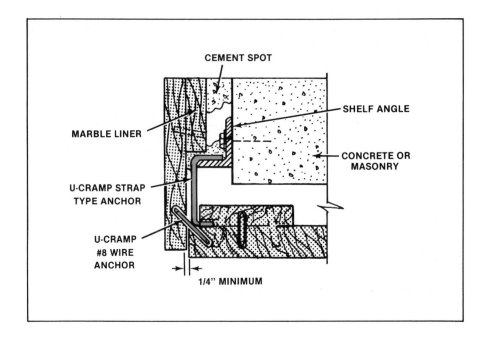

Figure 4-18
U-cramp strap and marble liner soffit anchor.

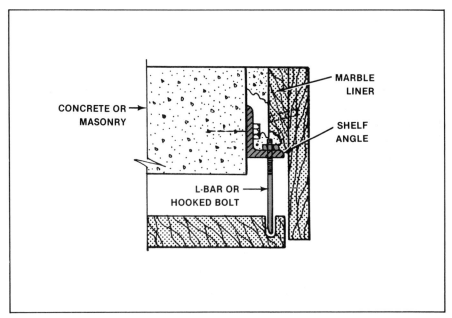

Figure 4-19
L-Bar or hooked bolt soffit anchor.

4.3 Framing

One of the latest methods used in stone construction is the use of frames. A framing system is nothing more than a rigid support for more than one piece of slab stone that is then attached to the building.

A possible alternative to attaching stone individually would be to plan a framing schedule. Framing of stone veneer consists of developing a steel frame system, usually built of tubular steel welded and/or bolted so as to form a single large panel or frame to which the individual stones are attached. The size of the frame is limited only by the intricacies of the actual design of the building and the lifting capacity of available cranes. The architect/engineer

Table 4.1 Strength of Standard Veneer Anchors in Marble and Granite

ANCHOR TYPE		SHEAR STRENGTH (lbs/anchor)	PULL-OUT STRENGTH (lbs/anchor)	RECOMMENDED SAFE LOADING (Safety Factor = 5 or greater)	
				WALL VENEER (lbs/anchor)	SOFFIT (lbs/anchor)
$1/2$" Diam. Rod		4375	875	800	170
Dovetail "L" Strap in		3370	870	600	170
"Z" Strap in Brick		3400	2000	600	400
#8 Gauge Cooper Wire in Brick[1]		3830	230	600	40
#8 Gauge Copper Wire in Concrete Block[1]		3540	100	600	20
"L" Strap with $1/4$" Dowel[2]		3100	1750	600	350
$3/8$" Lewis Key[3]		1400	2400	250	480

This table is based on laboratory studies conducted by IITRI, Carrara Marble, and the Canadian Standards Association publication *Connectors for Masonry*.

[1] The same recommended loading may be used for twisted, looped, and hooked #8 gauge wire anchors.

[2] Extrapolated values.

[3] Tested in granite.

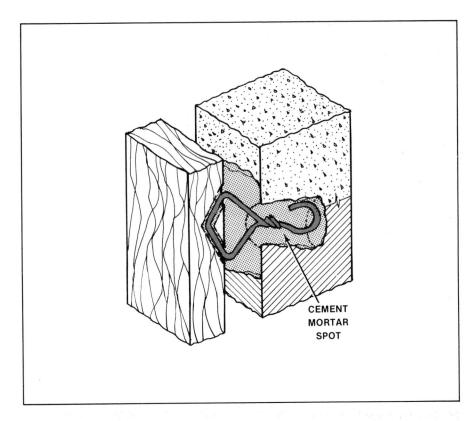

CEMENT
MORTAR
SPOT

Figure 4–20
Intermediate lace or belly tie anchor.

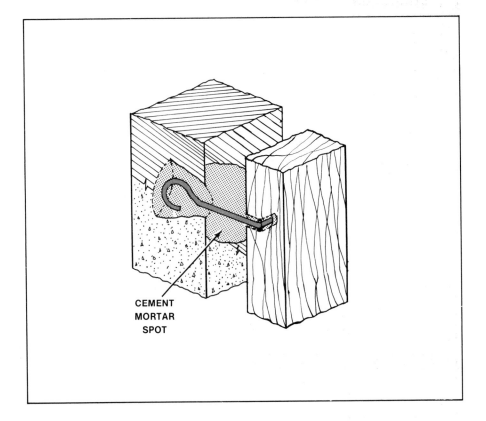

CEMENT
MORTAR
SPOT

Figure 4–21
Open edge anchor detail.

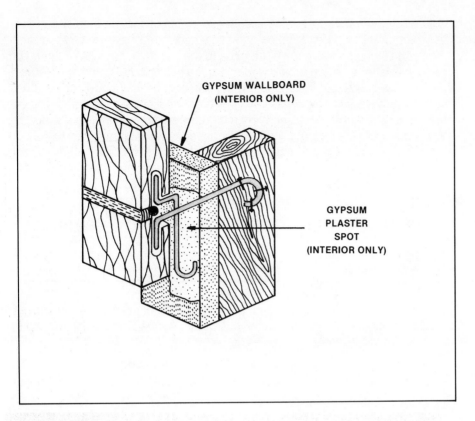

Figure 4–22
Anchoring marble to wood stud (interior detail).

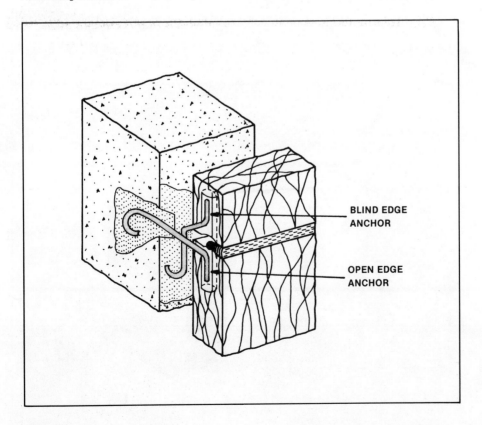

Figure 4–23
Connection of blind edge with open edge.

will design the frame system considering all potential movements due to temperature, creep and deformation and allow necessary clearances for attachment. The stone panels can be attached to the frame in the construction yard or shop or after erection of the frame onto the building. Next, the entire frame panel is transported to the job site where it is hoisted into place and attached to the structural system, usually by bolting or welding to the building. The entire process is similar to assembling a large three-dimensional jigsaw puzzle. The variety of possible approaches to assembling a framing system is so large that it is impossible to fully describe them all in a book; instead, some typical framing systems are shown with typical anchoring details in a broad brush approach (see Figures 4–24 through 4–27).

A framing specialist should be consulted on any framing job to assure that no criteria have been left out of the design. The criteria of main importance have been previously mentioned in other chapters. These are shrinkage, deformation, deflections, creep, the potential for water penetration and absorption, the galvanic action of dissimilar metalic contacts, and factors of safety for the entire design.

The anchoring system may also be designed using non-continuous extruded aluminum anchors in continuous or non-continuous slots in the stone, as shown in Figures 4–28 and 4–29.

Another method of attaching thin stone slab veneer is with concrete liners. This is simply a poured concrete liner on the back of thin stone with

Figure 4–24

Frame with continuous aluminum anchors.

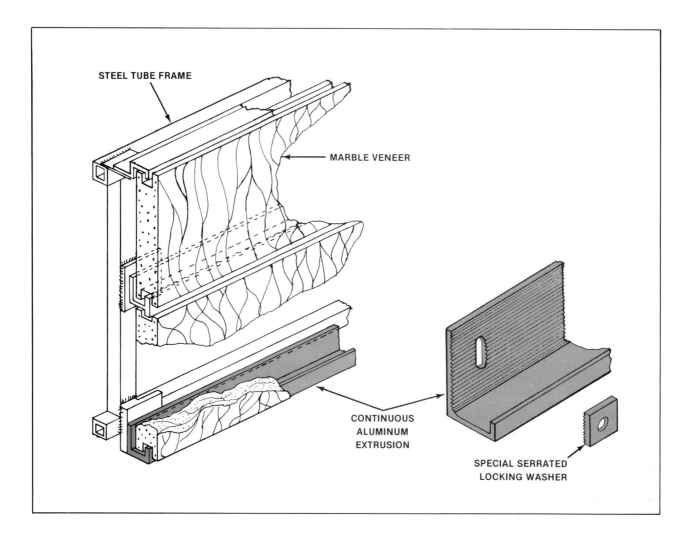

STEEL TUBE FRAME

MARBLE VENEER

CONTINUOUS
ALUMINUM
EXTRUSION

SPECIAL SERRATED
LOCKING WASHER

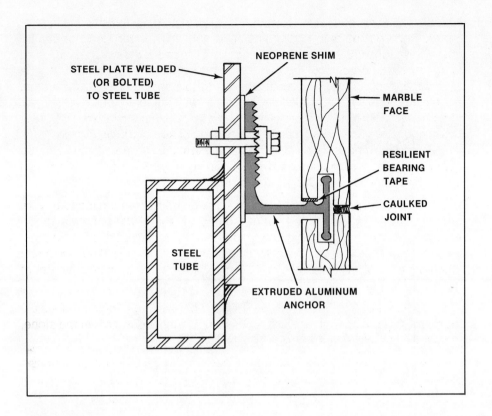

Figure 4-25
Extruded aluminum anchor with bearing point.

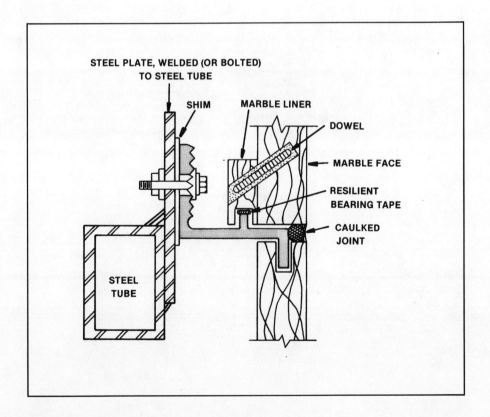

Figure 4-26
Extruded aluminum offset anchor.

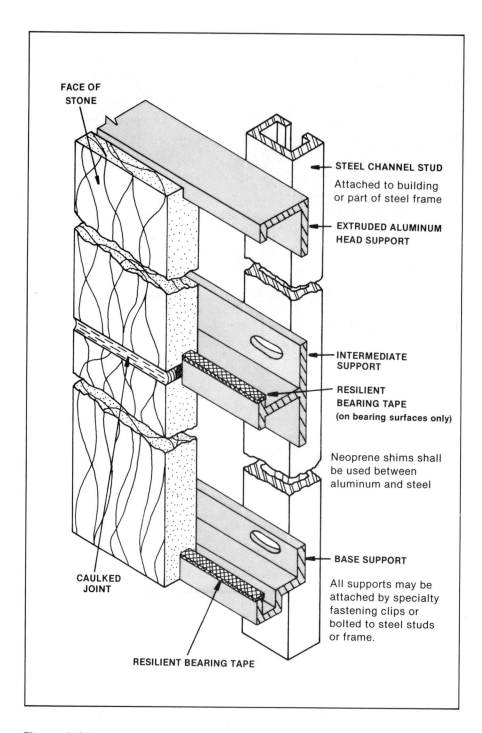

Figure 4–27
Continuous extruded aluminum anchors in continuous slots cut in the stone.

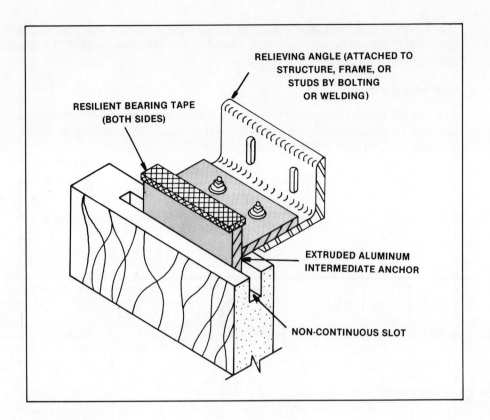

RELIEVING ANGLE (ATTACHED TO STRUCTURE, FRAME, OR STUDS BY BOLTING OR WELDING)

RESILIENT BEARING TAPE (BOTH SIDES)

EXTRUDED ALUMINUM INTERMEDIATE ANCHOR

NON-CONTINUOUS SLOT

Figure 4–28
Intermediate anchor in non-continuous slot.

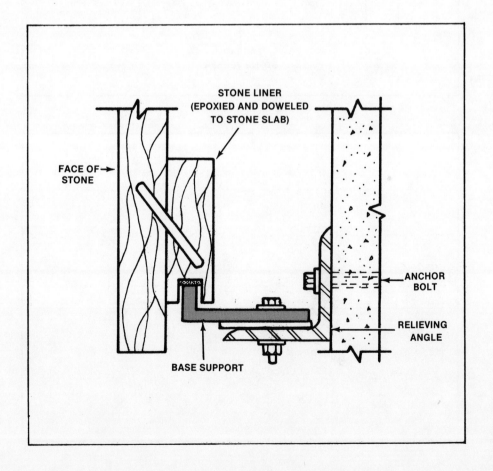

STONE LINER (EPOXIED AND DOWELED TO STONE SLAB)

FACE OF STONE

ANCHOR BOLT

RELIEVING ANGLE

BASE SUPPORT

Figure 4–29
Non-continuous extruded aluminum base support.

No. 8 non-ferrous wire anchors or specialty stone anchors connecting the concrete to the stone (see Figures 4–30 and 4–31). The advantage of this system is the use of thinner stone slabs.

4.4 Hardware

The marble and granite stone industry has developed accepted connection devices for anchoring stone slabs to any structure. A sampling of these devices is illustrated in Figure 4–32.

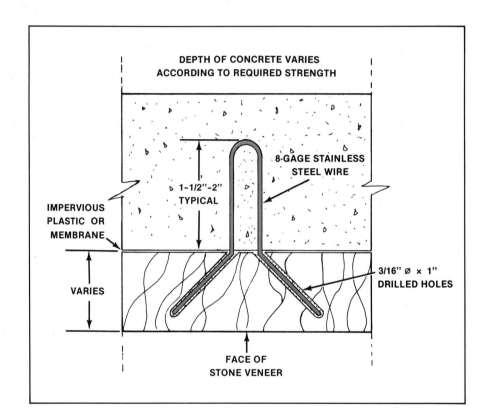

Figure 4–30

Pre-cast concrete liner with stone veneer facing.

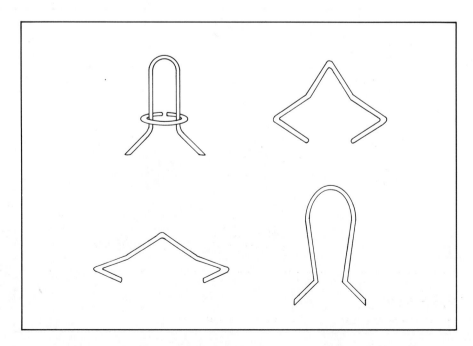

Figure 4–31

Typical pre-cast concrete stone anchors (sizes vary).

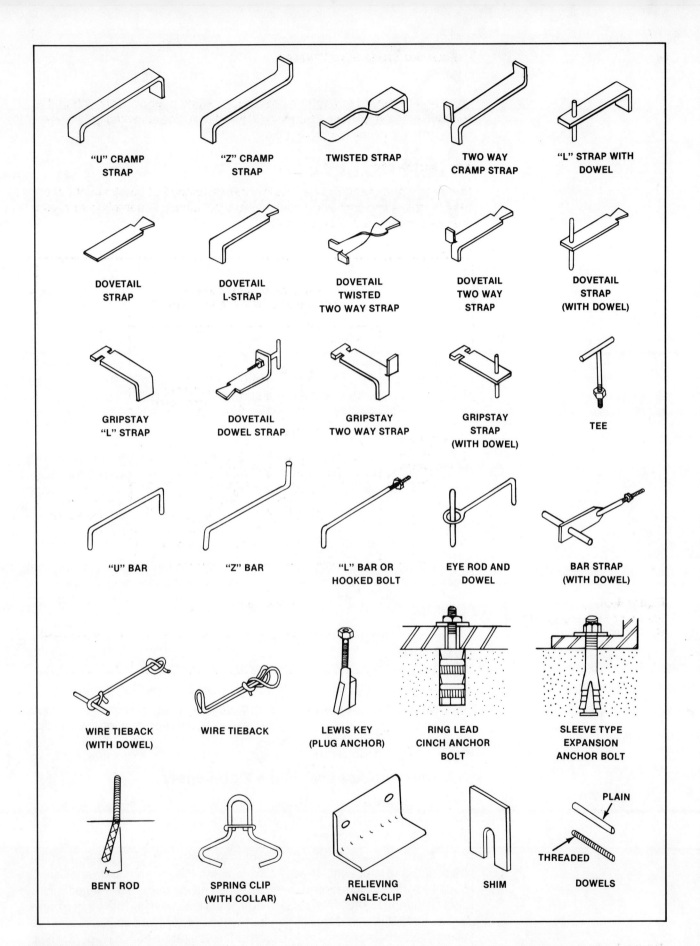

Figure 4-32
Some typical standard anchors and accessories.

65

5

Adhered Veneer

Adhered veneer is typically used for interior work, and only rarely for exterior applications. Adhered veneer is secured through adhesion to an approved bonding material applied over an approved backing (see Figure 5–1).

5.1 Adhered Veneer Codes

The application of adhered stone slab veneer must conform to applicable building codes and standards. The 1985 Uniform Building Code has minimum requirements, stated in this Section, that must be met to provide a safe structure.

5.1.1 Backing

The backing to which stone slab veneer is adhered must be continuous. The backing surface must be capable of securing and supporting the imposed loads of veneer. Exterior backing, including the stone veneer, must be weatherproof.

5.1.2 Size

As per the Uniform Building Code, individual adhered stone slab veneer units cannot exceed three feet in the greatest dimension no more than five square feet in area; the veneer cannot weigh more than 15 pounds per square foot. Size and weight limitations may be amended with approval of the building official.

5.2 Applying Adhered Stone Slab Veneer

Veneer may also be applied using one of the methods described in the Uniform Building Code, Section 3005. Refer to Figures 5–2 and 5–3 when reading the following procedures.

A paste of neat Portland cement is brushed onto the backing and the back of the veneer units. (Neat Portland cement is cement and water only.) Type S mortar is then applied to the backing and the back of the veneer units. Sufficient mortar should be used to create a slight excess. This slight excess will be forced out the edges of the units when they are tapped into place. The slightly excessive mortar and tapping of the veneer units into place will help to insure bond over the entire back surface area of the units. The mortar should be between ½'' and 1¼'' thick.

66

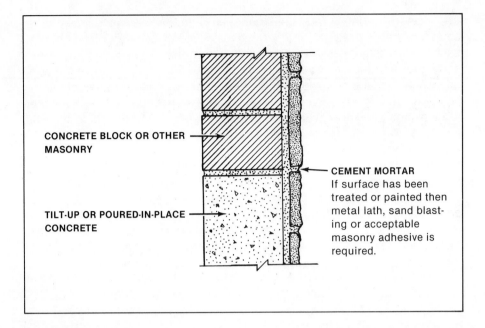

CONCRETE BLOCK OR OTHER MASONRY

TILT-UP OR POURED-IN-PLACE CONCRETE

CEMENT MORTAR
If surface has been treated or painted then metal lath, sand blasting or acceptable masonry adhesive is required.

Figure 5–1
Thin stone veneer on masonry or concrete wall.

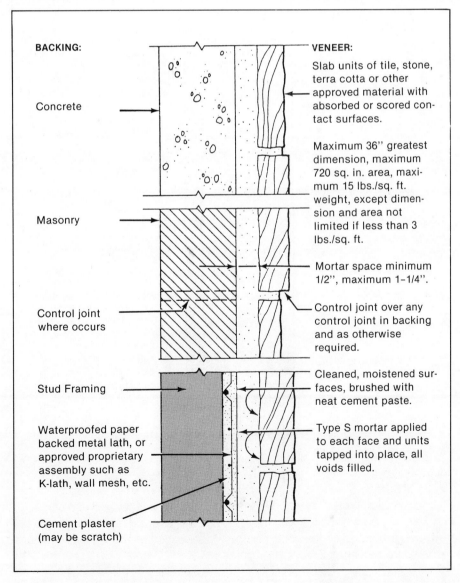

BACKING:

Concrete

Masonry

Control joint where occurs

Stud Framing

Waterproofed paper backed metal lath, or approved proprietary assembly such as K-lath, wall mesh, etc.

Cement plaster (may be scratch)

VENEER:

Slab units of tile, stone, terra cotta or other approved material with absorbed or scored contact surfaces.

Maximum 36'' greatest dimension, maximum 720 sq. in. area, maximum 15 lbs./sq. ft. weight, except dimension and area not limited if less than 3 lbs./sq. ft.

Mortar space minimum 1/2'', maximum 1–1/4''.

Control joint over any control joint in backing and as otherwise required.

Cleaned, moistened surfaces, brushed with neat cement paste.

Type S mortar applied to each face and units tapped into place, all voids filled.

Figure 5–2
Wall section.

Adhered stone veneer units not over 1'' in thickness and less that 81 square inches in area (9'' × 9'') can be adhered by using Portland cement. Larger units may be used if the back side of each unit is ground or box screeded to true up any deviations from plane. This helps assure full bond and avoids lippage. The backing can be concrete, Portland cement plaster on metal lath, or other masonry. The metal lath must be securely fastened to the supports by approved methods (see Chapter 47 of the Uniform Building Code). A setting bed of Portland cement mortar conforming to Table 30-A of the Uniform Building Code shall be applied to the backing. The setting bed will be a minimum ⅜'' thick and a maximum of ¾'' thick. A paste of neat Portland cement or half Portland cement and half graded sand is applied to the back of the veneer unit and to the setting bed. The veneer is then pressed and tapped into the setting bed to ensure complete coverage between the mortar bed and the veneer unit. Since this method does not force any excess mortar out the side of the veneer unit, Portland cement grout is used to point the veneer.

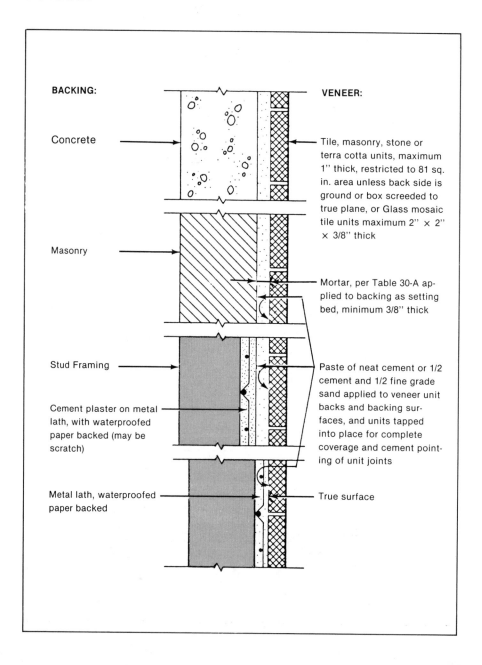

Figure 5-3
Wall section.

5.3 Wall and Floor Joints

When a stone slab veneer wall meets a marble or stone floor, the wall slab should be designed to rest on the finished floor, as shown in Figure 5–4. If the flooring is not stone, the stone veneer wall will continue below the finished floor line and the floor material will abut the face of the wall, as shown in Figure 5–5.

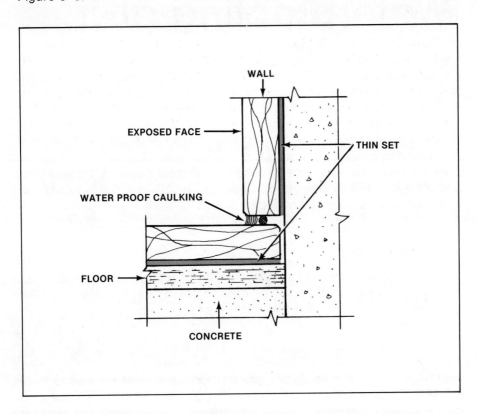

Figure 5–4
Detail of stone veneered wall and stone floor.

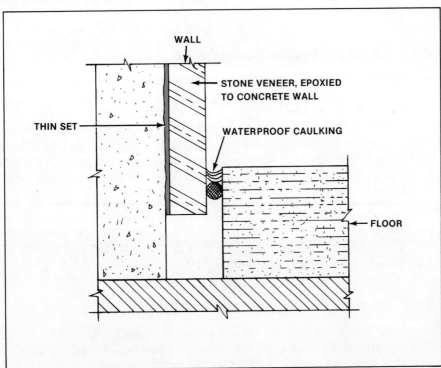

Figure 5–5
Detail of stone veneer wall meeting non-veneered floor.

6

Cleaning, Waterproofing and Protection

Marble and granite have been used for the most beautiful and endearing structures man has ever known; their fine quality and durability fulfill the modern designers' needs perfectly.

6.1 Cleaning

Any structure requires regular maintenance cleaning after construction and during its performance life. Stone veneer is susceptible to many of the same polutants as other building materials.

During construction, the primary rule of cleaning is "keep it clean." Prevention will save time spent on cures and remedies, especially since damages to granite and marble may be irreparable. Past experience shows that sometimes the cure is worse than the problem if proper care is not taken, so when cleaning marble, no acids or harsh abrasive cleaners or steel wire brushes should be used.

6.1.1 Cleaning Polished Surface Finishes

The type of stone finish will pretty much dictate the required cleaning method. A polished stone has a smooth, glossy finished surface that reflects light and emphasizes the color and markings of the stone. Polished marble finishes are traditionally used for interior wall veneers; their use is generally avoided in exterior applications due to their relative susceptibility to damage by airborne acids and wind-driven dust. Polished granite is not as susceptible to airborne acids. Many beautiful structures have been built using exterior polished finishes with clever architectural designs.

A regular maintenance schedule including periodic washing with clean potable water should be required. If slightly stronger cleaning is required, a mildly alkaline soapless cleaner may also be used. A soapless cleaner will help reduce the chances of streaking and filming.

6.1.2 Cleaning Honed Surface Finishes

Honed marble or granite have satin surfaces with relatively little light reflection and are typically used where a muted sheen will enhance the decor. Honed finished marbles are often used as exterior veneers.

Stone is porous by its very nature, but a honed finish is slightly more porous and absorptive than a polished finish and is generally more susceptible to soiling than polished finishes. Conversely, a honed finish is easier to restore because it will sustain harsher cleaning efforts.

A normal maintenance schedule should involve washing with clean potable water and a moderately abrasive cleaner, again mildly alkaline soapless cleaners are preferred.

6.1.3 Cleaning Special Surface Finishes

Sometimes the architect will want a special finish with distinctive textures for exceptional lighting effects, decor enhancement, graffiti-resistance and maintenance-reduction. The architect then uses a specialty finish.

Specialty finishes are surface finishes other than polished or honed and are often provided by individual marble and granite contractors under specific trade names, e.g., Velvet Finished and Bush Hammered. These specialty finishes are generally provided to satisfy requirements of service where a traditional polished or honed finish would prove inadequate, be subjected to unusual hazards, or not satisfy the architects' requirements.

Cleaning of specialty finishes will vary with its porosity and susceptibility to damage. The same practices used for polished and honed finishes are generally satisfactory for specialty finishes, however, the supplying marble contractor has the best information for cleaning and maintaining his specialty finish.

6.1.4 Poultice Method of Cleaning

Many stains can be removed by the use of a poultice or paste made with a solvent or regent and an inert material. The regent, such as Wyndott, Fawcett, or hydrogen peroxide, dissolves the stain. The dissolved stain and solvent are then leached into the poultice by an inert material such as Fuller's Earth. After the poultice has dried (approximately 48 hours), the powdery substance remaining is brushed off. Repeated applications may be required. The poultice method of stain removal prevents the stain from spreading by actually pulling the offensive material from the pores of the stone.

6.1.5 Periodic Cleaning Maintenance

The ideal in maintaining marble and granite veneers is to clean them at periodic intervals (e.g., annually), depending on the atmospheric conditions, by simply washing down with clean water. This will prevent the accumulation of dirt and impurities.

6.1.6 Harsher Cleaning

Sometimes none of the methods previously mentioned will satisfactorily clean the stone and a harsher cleaning method may be required. Using a method of cleaning harsher than those already mentioned will probably result in a change in the stone's appearance.

Sandblasting with fine, well-graded sand particles by air pressure or with sand and water mixed together and blasted onto the stone will remove almost any stain. Unfortunately, the abrasive action of the sand will also remove very small particles of the stone itself. This will open the pores of the stone, create a rougher finish, and change the appearance of the stone. The coarser finished stones will not be affected as much as the more highly finished, polished and honed stone surfaces.

The use of chemical cleaners also has the potential for cleaning almost any stain from stone. A chemical solution can be used to remove almost any stain from almost any type of stone. Special care must be taken to limit the spread of the solution to only those areas where it is required. A specialist in stone chemical cleaning should be contacted and a test panel used before actually cleaning the entire structure.

Cleaning with steam has also been done successfully. Care must be taken not to damage surrounding areas, especially gypsum plaster and wall board.

Before using any cleaning method, a test panel should be used to see if the method works, and especially to check for any damage to the stone itself.

6.2 Waterproofing

As man has progressed, he has, unfortunately, created conditions in the environment that can prove damaging to construction materials, even stone.

We have learned that by waterproofing, or more accurately by applying water repellents, such as silicons, we can prevent damaging pollutants from entering stone veneer and can maintain the natural beauty of the granite and marble.

Applying water repellents to the exterior face can help keep the wall looking dryer and cleaner for an extended period of time. Water repellents can be applied to veneer walls where there is no likelihood of water reaching the backsides of treated stones.

Granite and marble units should not be sealed on both faces (front and back) with waterproofing material as this would prevent the natural porous air flow in the stone, causing trapping of existing moisture. If the moisture that naturally exists in the stone unit cannot move, due to being sealed, freeze/thaw action will develop internal stresses that could prove damaging to the stone unit. Spalling could occur.

As with any application, exterior water repellents lose their effectiveness with time (sublimation) and weathering and will have to be reapplied. There is also a possibility of the water repellent material reacting to ultraviolet light, or the water repellent material may oxidize, resulting in discoloration of the coating. The manufacturer's representative should be consulted for application coverage and warranties.

6.3 Protection

Architects have long been aware of the necessity to design their structures with the possibilities of damage from the forces of nature and the destructive tendencies of man (vandalism). The prime reason stone was first used was because of its great durability and, of course, its beauty. Although surface protective films have generally fallen into disfavor for construction uses, they are still used to preserve stone statuary and many art treasures where ease of maintenance exists and cost is of minor concern. Though marble and

Figure 6-1
Fine example of a well-preserved stone masonry chapel in Orange, California.

granite are tough and have almost immeasurable durability, they can sometimes use a little extra protection. Hence, protective coatings have been used for centuries, such as waxes and parafin.

In modern construction, the application of a protective surface film on the surface of stone was quite usual until recently. Some protective films have tended to discolor (yellow) with age, usually within 10 to 15 years. It also must be remembered that any protective coating is a sacrificial item and will have to be reapplied on a regular basis to maitain its reliability.

This is not to say that a surface protective film should not be used, only that consideration should be given as to where it would do the most good, such as high traffic areas, and have a ready access for periodic maintenance. If a repellent is desired, a clear silicon application can be considered.

A test panel should always be made prior to actual application of any material to the structure itself.

7
Cut Stone Veneer Specification

Section 04450
Cut Stone Veneer

Part 1 General

1.01 Work Included

A. Cut [marble] [granite] [limestone] [_____] veneer at [exterior] [interior] wall.

B. Metal anchors [, mortar, and joint pointing.]

C. [Joint sealant.]

1.02 Work Installed but Furnished Under Other Sections

A. Section 05500—Metal Fabrications: Metal fabricated items for building into the work.

B. [Section 07620—Sheet Metal Flashing and Trim: Sheet metal coping and sill flashings.]

1.03 Work Furnished but Installed Under Other Sections

> **List Sections which install products furnished under this Section. When loose products or special equipment are to be installed "by Others," outside the Contract, it is considered that they will be installed "by Owner."**

A. Furnish wall anchors and devices to Section [_____] for placement.

1.04 Related Work

A. Section [_____—_____]: Concrete supporting wall.

> **Mortar can be included in this Section or can be referenced to the following Section.**

B. [Section 04100—Mortar: Bedding and pointing mortar].

C. Section [_____—_____]: Masonry supporting wall.

D. Section [05100—Structural Steel] [_____—_____]: Attachment anchorage from structural steel framing members.

E. Section 05500—Metal Fabrications: Shelf [angles] [_____] and supports.

F. Section [_____—_____]: [Formed steel] [Wood] framed supporting wall.

G. Section [_____—_____]: Water repellant coating.

H. Section 07620—Sheet Metal Flashing and Trim: Coping and sill flashings.

> **Sealants can be included in this Section or referenced to Section 07900.**

I. Section 07900—Joint Sealers: Sealant for [perimeter] [control] [expansion] joints.

1.05 References

> **Include only reference standards that are to be indicated within the text of this Section. Refer to TAS Section 04450. Edit the following, adding and deleting as required for project and product selection.**

A. [ANSI/ASTM C387—Packaged, Dry, Combined Materials for Mortar and Concrete.]

B. ASTM A36—Structural Steel

C. ASTM A123—Zinc (Hot Galvanized) Coatings on Products Fabricated from Rolled, Pressed, and Forged Steel Shapes.

D. [ASTM C270—Mortar for Unit Masonry.]

E. ASTM C503—Marble Building Stone (Exterior).

F. ASTM C615—Granite Building Stone.

G. ASTM C616—Sandstone Building Stone.

H. ASTM C629—Slate Building Stone.

1.06 Mockup

Use this Article for full sized erected assemblies required for review of construction, coordination of work of several Sections, testing, or observation of operation.

A. Provide mockup under provisions of Section [01400.] [01405.]

B. Size: [_____ × _____] feet ([_____ × _____] m).

C. Include cut stone, structural supporting wall, anchors, [control joint condition,] [window and accessories,] and [_____.]

1.07 Quality Assurance

A. Stone Supplier: Company specializing in quarrying cut stone with [ten] [_____] years experience.

B. Installer: Company specializing in installing cut stone [with [_____] years [documented] experience.] [approved by manufacturer.]

C. Design anchors and supports under direct supervision of experienced Professional Engineer, registered in State of [_____.]

1.08 Submittals

A. Submit shop drawings and product data under provisions of Section [01300.] [01340.]

B. Indicate on shop drawings, layout, pertinent dimensions, anchorages, [reinforcement,] head, jamb, and sill opening details, and [control] [expansion] jointing methods.

C. Provide product data on stone units, mortar products, [sealants,] reinforcements, and [_____.]

Use the following two Paragraphs for submission of physical samples for selection of finish, color, texture, etc.

D. Submit samples under provisions of Section [01300.] [01340.]

E. Submit [two] [_____] samples [_____ × _____] inch ([_____ × _____] mm) in size illustrating minimum and maximum sizes, color range and texture, markings, surface finish, and [_____.]

> **When manufacturers' instructions for specific installation requirements are utilized, carefully edit PART 3 EXECUTION requirements to avoid conflict with those instructions.**

F. Submit manufacturer's installation instructions and field erection or setting drawings under provisions of Section [01300.] [01340.]

G. [Indicate on setting drawings, panel identifying marks and locations.]

1.09 Delivery, Storage, and Handling

A. Deliver products to site under provisions of Section [1600.] [01610.]

B. Store and protect products under provisions of Section [01600.] [01620.]

> **Resting stone on wood timber supports at the jobsite prior to erection is an example of imposing stains directly to stone materials. Specify a temporary storage method conducive to the stone material specified. Storing stone panels vertically, resting weight on the panel edge, is a preferred method over laying panels flat and stacking.**

C. Store stone panels [vertically resting weight on panel edge.] [_____.]

D. Protect stone from visible discoloration.

1.10 Environmental Requirements

A. Maintain materials and surrounding air to a minimum 40 degrees F (5 degrees C) prior to, during, and 48 hours after completion of work.

B. During temporary storage on site, at the end of working day, or during rainy weather, cover stone work exposed to weather with nonstaining waterproof coverings, securely anchored.

Part 2 Products

2.01 Acceptable Stone Suppliers

> **Edit this Article if a stone supplier is identifiable. If only one supplier is acceptable, list in Article 2.02 and delete this Article; if more than one, list in this Article. If product substitution procedure is used, include Paragraph D. Refer to TAS Section 04450.**

A. [_____ .]

B. [_____ .]

C. [_____ .]

D. Substitutions: Under provisions of Section [01600.] [01630.]

Edit the following descriptive specifications for any conflicts with supplier's products specified above.

2.02 Stone

A. Limestone: [Cut Indiana Oolitic Limestone.] [_____.]

If a travertine stone is selected from the paragraph below, indicate whether it is filled or unfilled. Surface finishes vary considerably between different stone materials; specify accordingly. When two or more surface finishes are required, consider using a schedule at the end of this Section.

B. Marble: ASTM C503, Classification [I—Calcite;] [II—Dolomite;] [III—Serpentine;] [IV—Travertine;] [with [filled] [unfilled] surface.]

C. Granite: ASTM C615, [sawed.] [cut.] [split.] [_____.]

D. Slate: ASTM C629, Classification [I—Exterior;] [II—Interior;] [sawed.] [cut.] [split.] [_____.]

E. Sandstone: ASTM C616, Classification [I—Sandstone.] II—Quartzitic Sandstone.] [II—Quartzite.]

F. Color: [_____].

G. Surface Finish: [_____.]

H. Grade: [_____;] free of defects.

I. Thickness: [_____] inch ([_____] mm) nominal.

J. Face Size: [_____ × _____] inch ([_____ × _____] mm) nominal.

2.03 Mortar

Mortar can be referenced to Section 04100 or can be specified in this Section. If special mortar type or color is required, edit accordingly. Different setting and pointing mortars can be used; refer to Article 2.05.

A. Mortar: As specified in Section 04100.

[OR]

B. Mortar: ASTM C270 Type [M] [S] [N] [O] using [proportion] [property] specifications; with Type [I] [_____] Portland cement of [grey] [white] color [, with Type [S] [SA] hydrated lime.]

C. Water: Clean and potable.

> **Plasticizers, accelerators, retardants, water repellant agents or other admixtures are not recommended for mortar unless required by special conditions. If admixtures are necessary, consult manufacturers and evaluate products.**

D. Admixtures: [_____.]

> **Specify mortar color pigment when possible. Costs vary between available colors. Confirm that the selected color is compatible with the stone material and not a possible source of staining.**

E. Pointing Mortar Color: [Mineral oxide pigment] [_____] of [_____] color; [_____] manufactured by [_____.]

2.04 Accessories

> **Give serious consideration to the metal type used for anchoring and supporting stone work. Plain steel or coated steel have a limited life span compared to stainless or galvanized steel. Cavity spaces in exterior wall construction are subject to constant wetting and drying cycles. Stainless or *non-ferrous metal or* galvanized steel, providing the zinc coating is not removed or cracked during the wire twisting process, can offer longer life expectancy.**

A. Anchors, Dowels, Ties, Cramps, and [_____]: [Stainless steel, Type 304;] [Steel, ASTM A36, galvanized after fabrication to ASTM A123 [1.25] [_____] oz/sq ft ([380] [_____] g/sq m);] of sizes and configurations required for support of stone and applicable superimposed loads.

B. Supports: [Stainless steel, Type 304.] [Steel, ASTM A36, galvanized after fabrication to ASTM A123, [1.25] [_____] oz/sq ft ([380] [_____] g/sq m).]

C. Bolts, Washers, and Nuts: [Galvanized steel.] [Stainless steel, Type 304.] [_____.]

> **Select a flashing material that will not bleed or stain the stone finish or color.**

D. [Flashings: [[_____] type.] [Furnished under Section 07620.]]

> **The maximum lifting weight with hooks is usually determined by local union or trade practice.**

E. Lifting Hooks: Removable type [for panels in excess of [75] [_____]
lbs ([34] [_____] kg).]

> **Do not use an organic material for setting buttons; it can subsequently stain the stone or mortar during wetting and drying cycles.**

F. Setting Buttons: [Lead.] [Plastic.]

> **Include cavity vents only when applicable. Select an inorganic type, not subject to corrosion. Select type that will not permit insects to invade the cavity space.**

G. Cavity Vents: [_____] type; [_____] size; [_____] manufactured by [_____.]

> **Select one of the following two specifying methods. The second method requires identification of sealant attributes. Refer to Section 07900 for assistance. Select a sealant type that is stainless to the type and color of stone selected.**

H. Sealant: [[_____] Type specified in Section 07900, not detrimental to stone work.] [[_____] Type manufactured by [_____].]

> **A bituminous back coating is only practical on smooth stone surfaces and on stone which may readily absorb moisture. Consider coating back surface of porous stone veneer used at exterior walls where veneer is exposed to freeze and thaw cycling. Confirm advisability of back coating with stone supplier.**

I. Back Coating: [Bituminous.] [_____.]

J. Cleaning Solution: Type which will not harm stone, joint materials, or adjacent surfaces. Consult stone supplier for recommended type.

2.05 Mortar Mix

> **Pointing mortar should be weaker mix than setting mortar, so as to not transfer compressive stresses within the wall to the edge of the stone and cause spalling of the stone or fracture of the mortar.**

A. Provide Type [_____] setting mortar and Type [_____] pointing mortar.

B. Thoroughly mix mortar ingredients in quantities needed for immediate use.

C. Add [mortar color] [and] [admixtures] in accordance with manufacturer's instructions. Ensure uniformity of mix and coloration.

D. Do not use anti-freeze compounds in mortar.

E. Use mortar within two hours after mixing.

F. If necessary, retemper mortar within two hours of mixing to replace water lost by evaporation.

2.06 Stone Fabrication

Review setting procedures and setting and pointing requirements with stone supplier as it may affect fabrication of stone materials.

A. Form external corners to [quirk] [square] [_____] joint profile.

B. Slope exposed top surfaces of stone and horizontal sill surfaces for natural wash.

If drip slots are not shown on Drawings, include the following Paragraph.

C. Cut drip slot in work projecting more than ½ inch (13 mm) over [window frames] [_____.] Size slot not less than ⅜ inch (10 mm) wide and ¼ inch (6 mm) deep for full width of projection.

D. Coat [back] [cavity] surface of stone with [bituminous] [_____] back coating to surfaces not in contact with mortar. Allow coating to cure.

Part 3 Execution

3.01 Inspection

A. Verify that support work and site conditions are ready to receive work of this Section.

B. Establish lines, levels, and coursing. Protect from disturbance.

C. Beginning of installation means acceptance of [existing conditions] [and] [support work.]

3.02 Preparation

Use the following Paragraph only when anchorages for support of stone will be imbedded in concrete or masonry, or supported on structural steel or wood framing.

A.　Supply sufficient quantity of anchorages to Section [＿＿＿＿] for placement.

B.　Verify that items built-in under other Sections are properly located and sized.

C.　Clean stone prior to erection. Do not use wire brushes or implements which will mark or damage exposed surfaces.

3.03　Installation

A.　[Erect stone in accordance with stone supplier's instructions and erection drawings.]

B.　Arrange stone pattern to provide a consistent joint width of [¼] [＿＿＿＿] inch ([6] [＿＿＿＿] mm) throughout.

C.　[Provide setting bed [and pointing] mortar in accordance with Section 04100.]

> **When variations to a full mortar setting method are used, edit Paragraph D accordingly.**

D.　Place setting buttons and set stone in full mortar setting bed to support stone over full bearing surface and to establish joint dimensions.

E.　Shore up units [until setting bed will maintain panel in position without movement.] [for [7] [＿＿＿＿] days after setting.]

F.　Fill dowel [, Lewis,] and lifting holes with mortar.

> **There can be three methods to complete the exposed stone joint. Setting bed with pointing mortar (Paragraph G); setting bed with mortar joint raked back and pointed with sealant (Paragraph H); or no setting bed (stone is structurally supported) with joints pointed with sealant (Paragraph I). Edit the following Paragraphs accordingly.**

G.　To accomodate pointing mortar, rake out joints ⅝ to ¾ inch (16 to 19 mm). Brush mortar joints clean.

[OR]

> **To establish sealant joint sizes, refer to Section 07900 for proper joint width/depth ratio. Always use a backer rod or bond breaker.**

H. Rake out joints [_____] inch ([_____] mm) to accommodate sealant and [backing rod.] [bond breaker.] Brush mortar joints clean.

[OR]

I. Install sealant and [backing rod] [bond breaker] at joints.

J. [Fill joints with pointing mortar. Pack and work into voids. Neatly tool surface to [concave] [raked] [_____] joint.]

K. Install flashings of longest practical length and seal watertight to back-up. Lap end joint minimum [6] [_____] inches ([150] [_____] mm) and seal watertight.

> **The following Paragraph requires venting of cavity spaces at top and bottom to pressure equalize the space and to dry out the stone veneer and cavity space from moisture.**

L. Install cavity vents in vertical joints immediately above horizontal flashings and supports and at top of cavity spaces to provide cavity space venting.

3.04 Tolerances

> **Tolerances can be an expensive requirement to the project. Be reasonable with tolerances. Glossy or reflecting surfaces of stone may require tighter tolerances than would be appropriate for flat or non-reflective surfaces.**

A. Positioning of Elements: Maximum ¼ inch (6 mm) from true position.

B. Maximum Variation from Plan of Wall: ¼ inch in 10 feet (6 mm in 3 m); ½ inch in 50 feet (13 mm in 15 m).

C. Maximum Variation Between Face Plane of Adjacent Panels: [¹⁄₁₆] [_____] inch ([1.5] [_____] mm).

D. Maximum Variation from Plumb: ¼ inch (6 mm) per story non-cumulative; ½ inch (13 mm) in any two stories.

E. Maximum Variation from Level Coursing: ⅛ inch in 3 feet (3 mm/m); ¼ inch in 10 feet (6 mm in 3 m); ½ inch (13 mm) maximum.

F. Maximum Variation of Joint Thickness: ⅛ inch in 3 feet 3 mm/m. [or ¼ the Joint Width, whichever is less.]

3.05 Cutting and Fitting

A. Obtain approval prior to cutting or fitting any item not so indicated on Drawings.

B. Do not impair appearance or strength of stone work by cutting.

3.06 Cleaning

A. Remove excess mortar [and sealant] upon completion of work.

B. Clean soiled surfaces with cleaning solution.

C. Use non-metallic tools in cleaning operations.

3.07 Schedule

> **Provide a schedule when stone surface finishes, colors, or textures vary for different locations.**

7.1 Code Standards

Sections of the 1988 Uniform Building Code and the 1988 California State Building Code are included to aid and clarify the use of slab stone veneer.

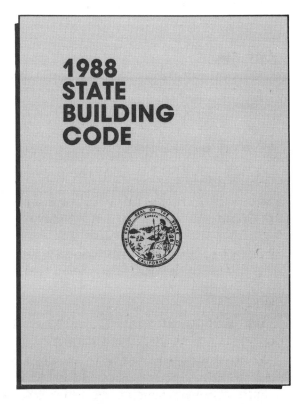

UNIFORM BUILDING CODE
Chapter 30
VENEER

Scope

Sec. 3001. (a) **General.** All veneer and its application shall conform to the requirements of this code. Wainscots not exceeding 4 feet in height measured above the adjacent ground elevation for exterior veneer or the finish floor elevation for interior veneer may be exempted from the provisions of this chapter if approved by the building official.

(b) **Limitations.** Exterior veneer shall not be attached to wood-frame construction at a point more than 30 feet in height above the noncombustible foundation, except the 30-foot limit may be increased when special construction is designed to provide for differential movement and when approved by the building official.

Definitions

Sec. 3002. For the purpose of this chapter, certain terms are defined as follows:

BACKING as used in this chapter is the surface or assembly to which veneer is attached.

VENEER is nonstructural facing of brick, concrete, stone, tile, metal, plastic or other similar approved material attached to a backing for the purpose of ornamentation, protection or insulation.

Adhered Veneer is veneer secured and supported through adhesion to an approved bonding material applied over an approved backing.

Anchored Veneer is veneer secured to and supported by approved mechanical fasteners attached to an approved backing.

Exterior Veneer is veneer applied to weather-exposed surfaces as defined in Section 424.

Interior Veneer is veneer applied to surfaces other than weather-exposed surfaces as defined in Section 424.

Materials

Sec. 3003. Materials used in the application of veneer shall conform to the applicable requirements for such materials as set forth elsewhere in this code.

For masonry units and mortar, see Chapter 24.

For precast concrete units, see Chapter 26.

For portland cement plaster, see Chapter 47.

Anchors, supports and ties shall be noncombustible and corrosion resistant.

When the terms "corrosion resistant" or "noncorrosive" are used in this chapter they shall mean having a corrosion resistance equal to or greater than a hot-dipped galvanized coating of 1.5 ounces of zinc per square foot of surface area. When an element is required to be corrosion resistant or noncorrosive, all of its parts shall be corrosion resistant, such as screws, nails, wire, dowels, bolts, nuts, washers, shims, anchors, ties and attachments.

Design

Sec. 3004. (a) **General.** The design of all veneer shall comply with the requirements of Chapter 23 and this section.

Veneer shall support no load other than its own weight and the vertical dead load of veneer above.

Surfaces to which veneer is attached shall be designed to support the additional vertical and lateral loads imposed by the veneer.

Consideration shall be given for differential movement of supports, including that caused by temperature changes, shrinkage, creep and deflection.

(b) **Adhered Veneer.** With the exception of ceramic tile, adhered veneer and its backing shall be designed to have a bond to the supporting element sufficient to withstand a shearing stress of 50 pounds per square inch.

(c) **Anchored Veneer.** Anchored veneer and its attachments shall be designed to resist a horizontal force equal to twice the weight of the veneer.

Anchored Veneer

Sec. 3006. (a) **Permitted Backing.** Backing may be of any material permitted by this code. Exterior veneer including its backing shall provide a weatherproof covering.

(b) **Height and Support Limitations.** Anchored veneers shall be supported on footings, foundations or other noncombustible support except as provided under Section 2515.

In Seismic Zones Nos. 2, 3 and 4 the weight of all anchored veneers installed on structures more than 30 feet in height above the noncombustible foundation or support shall be supported by noncombustible, corrosion-resistant structural framing. The structural framing shall have horizontal supports spaced not more than 12 feet vertically above the initial 30-foot height. The vertical spacing between horizontal supports may be increased when special design techniques, approved by the building official, are used in the construction.

Noncombustible, noncorrosive lintels and noncombustible supports shall be provided over all openings where the veneer unit is not self spanning. The deflections of all structural lintels and horizontal supports required by this subsection shall not exceed 1/600 of the span under full load of the veneer.

(c) **Area Limitations.** The area and length of anchored veneer walls shall be unlimited, except as required to control expansion and contraction and by Section 3001 (b).

(d) **Application.** In lieu of the design required by Section 3004 (a) and (c), anchored veneer may be applied in accordance with the following:

3. **Slab-type units (2 inches maximum in thickness).** For veneer units of marble, travertine, granite or other stone units of slab form, ties of corrosion-resistant metal shall engage drilled holes of corrosion-resistant metal dowels located in the middle third of the edge of the units spaced a maximum of 24 inches apart around the periphery of each unit with not less than four ties per veneer unit. Units shall not exceed 20 square feet in area.

If the dowels are not tight fitting, the holes may be drilled not more than 1/16 inch larger in diameter than the dowel with the hole countersunk to a diameter and depth equal to twice the diameter of the dowel in order to provide a tight-fitting key of cement mortar at the dowel locations when the mortar in the joint has set.

All veneer ties shall be corrosion-resistant metal capable of resisting in tension or compression a force equal to two times the weight of the attached veneer.

If made of sheet metal, veneer ties shall be not smaller in area than No. 22 gauge by 1 inch or, if made of wire, not smaller in diameter than No. 9 gauge wire.

STATE BUILDING CODE
(Part 2, Title 24, C.A.C.)
Chapter 30
VENEER

Scope

Sec. 3001. (a) General. All veneer and its application shall conform to the requirements of this code. Wainscots not exceeding 4 feet in height measured above the adjacent ground elevation for exterior veneer or the finish floor elevation for interior veneer may be exempted from the provisions of this chapter if approved by the enforcement agency.

NOTE: See Section 3007 for inspection requirements.

Sec. 3001. (b) Limitations. Exterior veneer shall not be attached to wood frame construction at a point more than 25 feet in height above the adjacent ground elevation except when approved by the enforcement agency considering special construction designed to provide for differential movement.

Where wood frame construction provides lateral support for veneer, studs or similar vertical load supporting members shall be continuous between the foundation and the top of the veneer.

Materials

Sec. 3003. Materials used in the application of veneer shall conform to the applicable requirements for such materials as set forth elsewhere in this code.

For masonry units and mortar, see Chapter 24.
For precast concrete units, see Chapter 26.
For portland cement plaster, see Chapter 47.

Anchors, supports and ties shall be noncombustible and corrosion resistant. When the terms "corrosion resistant" or "noncorrosive" are used in this chapter they shall mean having a hot-dipped galvanized coating of 1.5 ounces of zinc per square foot of the surface area. When an element is required to be corrosion resistant or noncorrosive all of its parts shall be corrosion resistant such as screws, nails, wire, dowels, bolts, nuts, washers, shims, anchors, ties and attachments.

Grout shall conform to the requirements of Section 2403(d)2 for fine grout.

Design

Sec. 3004 (a) General. The design of all veneer shall comply with the requirements of Chapter 23 and this section.

Veneer shall support no load other than its own weight and the vertical dead load of veneer above.

Surfaces to which veneer is attached shall be designed to support the additional vertical and lateral loads imposed by the veneer.

Consideration shall be given for differential movement of supports, including that caused by temperature changes, shrinkage, creep and deflection.

In no case shall veneer be considered as part of the wall in computing strength or deflection nor shall it be considered a part of the required thickness of the wall.

Veneer shall be anchored in a manner which will not allow relative movement between the veneer and the wall.

Adhered Veneer

Sec. 3005 (c) Unit Size Limitations. Veneer units shall not exceed 36 inches in the greatest dimension nor more than 720 square inches in total area and shall weigh not more than 15 pounds per square foot unless approved by the enforcement agency.

Units of tile, masonry, stone or terra cotta which exceed 1/2 inch in thickness shall be applied as for anchored veneer where used over exit ways or more than 20 feet in height above adjacent ground elevation.

EXCEPTION: Veneer units weighing less than 3 pounds per square foot shall not be limited in dimension or area.

Anchored Veneer

Sec. 3006 (d) Application. In lieu of the design required by subsection 3004(c) UBC, anchored veneer may be applied by any one of the methods specified below:

3. Slab Type Units Two Inches Maximum in Thickness. All veneer units of marble, travertine, granite or other stone units of slab form shall be 2 inches maximum in thickness and 1 1/4 inches in minimum thickness for exterior and 3/4 inch minimum thickness for interior use and shall be set a minimum of 1 inch clear of the backing, and the space shall be solidly filled with fine grout or each piece shall be set rigidly against spot bedding pads. Spot bedding pads shall be of cement mortar not less than 6 inches in diameter and shall be located at each anchor tie and over the back face of the veneer at a maximum spacing of 18 inches on center. The spot bedding at ties shall entirely surround the ties.

Ties shall engage drilled eyes of corrosion-resistant metal dowels of 1/8 inch diameter or more penetrating at least 1/2 inch into the edge of the veneer located in the middle third of the edge of the units spaced a maximum of 18 inches apart around the periphery of each unit with not less than four ties per veneer unit. Units shall not exceed 20 feet square in area.

If the dowels are not tight fitting, the holes may be drilled not more than 1/16 inch larger in diameter than the dowel with the hole countersunk to a diameter and depth equal to twice the diameter of the dowel in order to provide a tight-fitting key of cement mortar at the dowel locations when the mortar in the joint has set.

All veneer ties shall be corrosion-resistant metal capable of resisting in tension or compression a force equal to two times the weight of the attached veneer.

If made of sheet metal, veneer ties shall be not smaller in area than 1/16 inch by 1 inch, or if made of wire, not smaller in diameter than No. 9 gage wire.

Sec. 3006. (e) Unit Size Limitations. The thickness of anchored unit masonry and stone veneer including grout, shall be not less than 3 inches.

Inspection

Sec. 3006. All veneer shall be continuously inspected during application by an inspector specially approved for that purpose by the enforcement agency.

8

Technical Data, Testing and Standards

8.1 Stone Properties

Stones are a natural product of nature and as such have a wide variation in characteristics and strengths. Consistency between stones is not as reliable as consistency from manufactured building materials. This is an important concept to understand.

To use the building material as economically as possible, designers typically want their materials to be as thin and as light as reasonable. Using a natural material with the variations that stone has requires that a comparatively high factor of safety must be used. Normal factors of safety range from 3 for stones with uniform test values to as high as 10 for widely scattered test results.

Before any stone can be used on a building, it is important to know what its strength characteristics are. This would mean its modulus of rupture, its flexural strength and its compressive strength. Other information can be pertinent as well but these three are definitely required.

The American Society for Testing and Materials, Natural Building Stone Committee C–18 has developed standard test methods for natural building stones that can be used to determine stone strengths. These tests should be applied early in the design process so that the safest and most economical design can be developed. These values are usually obtainable from the stone supplier, however, sometimes additional testing is required by the designer.

8.1.1 Strength (ASTM C99, ASTM C170, ASTM C880)

Several factors affect the strength characteristics of stone, notably the veining or cleavages of the crystals in the stone, the amount of cohesion or interlocking of the crystals and the cementitious nature inherent in the stone.

8.1.2 Abrasion Resistance (ASTM C241-51 (20))

Designers often mix and match stones to create interesting paving patterns. Stone being a naturally hard material is ideal for this application, however, those stones with an abrasion hardness, Ha, or 10 or higher work the best for flooring materials.

When mixing stones Ha differences greater than 5 should be avoided otherwise non-uniform wearing patterns will appear in the paving.

8.1.3 Safety Factors

When testing a stone, the greater the variation in test results, the less reliable the stone will be, if there is very little deviation in test data then the stone can be used with confidence with a lower factor of safety. Commonly stones are designed with a factor of safety of about 5.

When stone is used in areas that are subjected to concentrated loadings such as stair treads or lintels a factor of safety as high as 10 may be used. These factors, of course, can be adjusted depending upon test data and engineering judgement.

Table 8.1 shows the range of physical properties for selected stones. The values are the results of tests done at the Illinois Institute of Technology Research Institute on 16 commercial American marbles, the range from 135 different Italian stones and National Bureau of Standards Reports.

8.2 Test Methods

The recommended tests for natural stone slab veneer are ASTM C-99 Test for Modulus of Rupture, and ASTM C-880 Test for Flexural Strength. Other valuable tests would be ASTM E-330 Structural Load Test by Uniform Static Pressure (positive and negative), ASTM E-283 Air Infiltration Test by Static Pressure, ASTM E-331 Water Infiltration Test by Static Pressure, and AAMA TM-1-76 Test for Water Penetration Using Dynamic Pressure. An anchor pullout test on the engineered anchoring system used would be helpful for the final detail designs.

When marble and stone are used for paving walkways, stairs and flooring, the abrasion resistance of the stone should also be tested in accordance with ASTM C-241 Abrasion Resistance of Stone Subjected to Foot Traffic.

Table 8.1 Range of Physical Properties of Stones					
PROPERTY	MARBLES (including travertine	GRANITE	LIME-STONE	SAND-STONE	SLATE
COMPRESSIVE STRENGTH(psi)	6,000–50,000	7,700–60,000	2,600–32,000	2,000–37,000	10,000–15,000
FLEXURAL STRENGTH(psi)	600–4,900	1430–5,500	400–2000	700–2,300	6,000–15,000
DENSITY (pcf)	142–184	159–190	110–185	135–170	170–190
MODULUS OF ELASTICITY (psi × 10^{-6})	1.97–19.0	2.0–10.0	0.6–1.4	1.0–1.75	
ABSORPTION (%)	0.069–0.609	0.02–0.40	0.6–12.0	1.0–20.0	
SPECIFIC GRAVITY	2.64–2.72	2.61–2.70	2.10–2.75	2.14–2.66	2.74–2.82
COEFFICIENT OF THERMAL EXPANSION (in/°F) × 10^{-6}	3.69–12.30	4.7(average)	4.4(average)	5.0–12.0	9.4–12.0

Designation: C 97 – 83$^{\epsilon 1}$

AMERICAN SOCIETY FOR TESTING AND MATERIALS
1916 Race St., Philadelphia, Pa. 19103
Reprinted from the Annual Book of ASTM Standards, Copyright ASTM
If not listed in the current combined index, will appear in the next edition.

Standard Test Methods for
ABSORPTION AND BULK SPECIFIC GRAVITY OF NATURAL BUILDING STONE[1]

This standard is issued under the fixed designation C 97; the number immediately following the designation indicates the year of original adoption or, in the case of revision, the year of last revision. A number in parentheses indicates the year of last reapproval. A superscript epsilon (ε) indicates an editorial change since the last revision or reapproval.

$^{\epsilon 1}$ NOTE—Section 4.1 was corrected editorially in May 1985.

1. Scope

1.1 These test methods cover the tests for determining the absorption and bulk specific gravity of all types of natural building stone. except slate.

1.2 The values stated in inch-pound units are to be regarded as the standard.

1.3 *This standard may involve hazardous materials, operations, and equipment. This standard does not purport to address all of the safety problems associated with its use. It is the responsibility of whoever uses this standard to consult and establish appropriate safety and health practices and determine the applicability of regulatory limitations prior to use.*

2. Significance and Use

2.1 These test methods are useful in indicating the differences in absorption between the various building stones. These test methods also provide one element in comparing stones of the same type.

ABSORPTION

3. Sampling

3.1 The sample shall be selected to represent a true average of the type or grade of stone under consideration and shall be of the quality supplied to the market under the type designation to be tested. The sample may be selected by the purchaser or his authorized representative from the quarried stone or taken from the natural ledge and shall be of adequate size to permit the preparation of at least three test specimens. When perceptible variations occur, the purchaser may select as many samples as are necessary for determining the range in properties.

4. Test Specimens

4.1 The specimens may be cubes, prisms, cylinders, or any regular form with least dimension not under 2 in. (50.8 mm) and greatest dimension not over 3 in., (76.2 mm) but the ratio of volume to surface area shall be not less than 0.3 in. (7.6 mm) nor greater than 0.5 in. (12.7 mm). All surfaces shall be reasonably smooth. Saw or core drill surfaces are considered satisfactory, but rougher surfaces shall be finished with No. 80 abrasive. No chisels or similar tools shall be used at any stage of preparing the specimens. At least three specimens shall be prepared from each sample.

5. Procedure

5.1 Dry the specimens for 24 h in a ventilated oven at a temperature of 105 ± 2°C (221 ± 3.6°F).

5.2 After drying, cool the specimens in the room for 30 min and weigh. When the specimens cannot be weighed immediately after cooling, store them in a desiccator. Determine the weights to the nearest 0.02 g.

5.3 Immerse the specimens completely in filtered or distilled water at 20 ± 5°C (68 ± 9°F) for 48 h. At the end of this period remove them from the water bath one at a time, surface dry

---

[1] These test methods are under the jurisdiction of ASTM Committee C-18 on Natural Building Stones and are the direct responsibility of Subcommittee C18.01 on Test Methods.

Current edition approved June 24, 1983. Published August 1983. Originally published as C 97 – 30. Last previous edition C 97 – 47 (1982).

C 97

with a damp cloth, and weigh to the nearest 0.02 g.

6. Calculations and Report

6.1 Calculate the weight percentage absorption (Note 1) for each specimen as follows:

$$\text{Absorption, weight \%} = [(B - A)/A] \times 100$$

where:
A = weight of the dried specimen, and
B = weight of the specimen after immersion.

NOTE 1—If the percentage of absorption by volume is desired it will be necessary to determine the bulk specific gravity and multiply each value of percentage absorption by weight by the corresponding bulk specific gravity value.

6.2 Report the average of all the specimens from each sample as the absorption of the sample. The report shall state the highest and lowest values and the average.

BULK SPECIFIC GRAVITY

7. Samples and Test Specimens

7.1 Samples may be the same as those used for absorption, or other samples may be selected in accordance with Section 3. At least three test specimens from each sample shall be tested, and they shall conform to the requirements of Section 4 as to size, shape, and preparation.

8. Procedure

8.1 When both absorption and bulk specific gravity are to be determined on the same specimens, weigh the saturated specimens suspended in filtered or distilled water at 20 ± 5°C (68 ± 9°F) immediately after the absorption tests are completed. Determine the suspended weights to the nearest 0.02 g. A satisfactory means of weighing specimens in water is to use a basket, similar to that illustrated in Fig. 1, for suspending the specimens in a glass jar of water supported above the balance pan. Determine the weight of the basket when suspended in water to the same depth as when weighing specimens therein. Subtract the weight of the basket to the nearest 0.02 g from the combined weight of the specimen and basket. Carefully remove air bubbles clinging to the basket or specimen before recording the weight.

8.2 When the bulk specific gravity test is made on specimens other than those used for absorption, determine the dry weights as in 5.1 and 5.2. Immerse the specimens in filtered or distilled water at 20 ± 5°C (68 ± 9°F) for at least 1 h or until air bubbles do not form on the specimens within 5 min. Surface dry the specimens as in 5.3, weigh to the nearest 0.02 g, and return to the water bath. Determine the weights in water before the specimens have stood in the water more than 5 min.

9. Calculations and Report

9.1 Calculate the bulk specific gravity as follows:

$$\text{Bulk specific gravity} = A/(B - C)$$

where:
A = weight of the dried specimen,
B = weight of the soaked and surface-dried specimen in air, and
C = weight of the soaked specimen in water.

9.2 Calculate the results to three decimal places and round off to two. Report the average, maximum, and minimum values.

NOTE 2—The bulk specific gravity gives a convenient and accurate means of calculating the unit weight of the stone; for example, weight per cubic foot (cubic metre) (dry stone) = bulk specific gravity × 62.4.

10. Precision and Bias

10.1 Individual variations in a natural product may result in deviation from accepted values. A precision section will be added when sufficient data are available to indicate in repeatability and reproducibility.

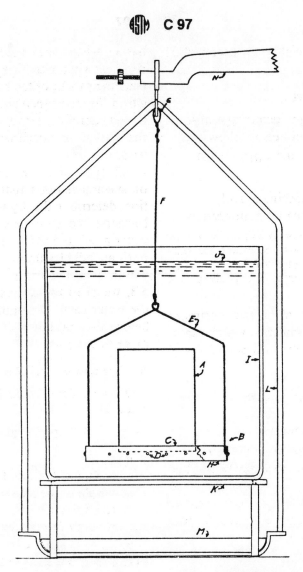

A—Specimen.
B—Suspension basket.
C—Brass ring.
D—Bottom of basket of No. 13 B & S gage (1.83 mm) brass wire (all joints soldered).
E—Bail of basket of No. 13 B & S gage (1.83 mm) brass wire.
F—Suspension wire of No. 20 B & S gage (0.812 mm) brass wire.
G—Loop for attachment to stirrup of balance

H—Cutaway section of basket.
I—Water jar.
J—Water level.
K—Water jar support.
L—Balance pan suspension rod.
M—Balance pan.
N—Beam of balance.

FIG. 1 Bulk Specific Gravity Test Assembly

Designation: C 99 – 52 (Reapproved 1981)[ε1]

AMERICAN SOCIETY FOR TESTING AND MATERIALS
1916 Race St., Philadelphia, Pa. 19103
Reprinted from the Annual Book of ASTM Standards, Copyright ASTM
If not listed in the current combined index, will appear in the next edition.

Standard Test Method for
MODULUS OF RUPTURE OF NATURAL BUILDING STONE[1]

This standard is issued under the fixed designation C 99; the number immediately following the designation indicates the year of original adoption or, in the case of revision, the year of last revision. A number in parentheses indicates the year of last reapproval. A superscript epsilon (ε) indicates an editorial change since the last revision or reapproval.

[ε1] NOTE—Editorial changes were made throughout in July 1984.

1. Scope

1.1 This test method covers the determination of the modulus of rupture of all types of natural building stone except slate.

2. Apparatus

2.1 *Testing Machine*—The accuracy of the testing machine shall be within 1 % for the range from 10 to 1000 lbf (44 to 4450 N).

2.2 *Knife Edges*—The supports for the specimen shall be two knife edges of the rocker type (Fig. 1) with edges at least as long as the width of the specimen. The loading knife edge may be of either the rocker or rigid type.

3. Sampling

3.1 Select the sample to represent a true average of the type or grade of stone under consideration and of the quality supplied to the market under the type designation to be tested. The sample may be selected by the purchaser or his authorized representative from the quarried stone or taken from the natural ledge and shall be of adequate size to permit the preparation of the desired number of test specimens. When perceptible variations occur, the pruchaser may select as many samples as are necessary for determining the variations in modulus of rupture.

4. Test Specimens

4.1 The specimens shall be approximately 4 by 8 by 2¼ in. (101.6 by 203.2 by 57.2 mm) in size, and three or more shall be prepared for each desired condition of loading. They shall be sawed from the sample and finished by grinding to smooth surfaces. The 4 by 8-in. faces shall be as nearly plane and parallel as practicable. For load-ing perpendicular to the rift (Note 1) three specimens shall be prepared with the 4 by 8-in. faces parallel to the rift planes (see A_2 in Fig. 1), and for loading parallel to the rift, three specimens shall be prepared with the 4 by 2¼-in. (101.6 by 57.2 mm) faces parallel to the rift (Note 2). When test are desired on the stone in both the wet and dry condition, six specimens shall be prepared for each direction of loading; that is, three for tests dry, perpendicular to the rift, three for tests wet, perpendicular to the rift, etc.

NOTE 1—The term rift is used here to designate the direction in which the stone splits most easily. In stratified stones it is considered to coincide with the bedding or stratification. The rift direction should always be marked on the sample by the quarryman, since it often is not possible to determine it on a small block.

NOTE 2—Another condition of loading may occur in structures when the rift planes are vertical and parallel to the length of the beam. The strength of the stone may be obtained for such loading by cutting the specimens with the 2¼ by 8-in. (57.2 by 203.2-mm) face parallel to the rift. The meager data available for this condition of loading indicates that the strength is at least as high as when the load is applied perpendicular to the rift as shown by A_2 in Fig. 1.

5. Marking and Measuring Specimens

5.1 On the 4 by 8-in. (101.6 by 203.2-mm) face draw the center line perpendicular to one edge (8 by 2¼-in. (203.2 by 57.2-mm) face) and extend down both edges perpendicular to the 4 by 8-in. face. At a distance of 3.5 in. (88.9 mm) each way from the center line, draw two similar sets of lines (span lines, "*a*" in Fig. 1). Mark each

[1] This test method is under the jurisdiction of ASTM Committee C-18 on Natural Building Stones and is the direct responsibility of Subcommittee C18.01 on Test Methods.

Current edition approved Sept. 30, 1952. Originally issued 1934. Replaces D 327 and C 99 – 47.

C 99

specimen to indicate the direction of the rift and label with suitable numbers or letters for identification in measuring and testing.

5.2 Measure the dimensions of the cross section on the center line. Measure the width to the nearest 0.01 in. (0.25 mm) and take the thickness as the average of three measurements to the nearest 0.01 in., one taken at the center and one near each edge.

6. Conditioning

6.1 Before testing the specimens for dry strength, dry them for 24 h at 105 ± 2°C (221 ± 3.6°F). Before testing the specimens for wet strength, immerse them for 48 h in water at 25 ± 5°C (77 ± 9°F).

7. Procedure

7.1 Lay the specimen flatwise on the supporting knife edges, spaced 7 in. (177.8 mm) apart and equidistant from the loading knife edges (Note 3), with all three knife edges parallel. When a load of 10 lbf (44 N) has been applied, stop the loading and make all knife edges coincide with the marks on the specimen by centering the specimen under the loading edge and moving the supporting edges under the span marks. Apply the loading at a rate not exceeding 1000 lbf/min (4450 N/min) until failure of the specimen.

NOTE 3—When all three knife edges are of the rocker type, care must be taken to adjust all three until the top face of the spcimen is horizontal when loaded.

8. Calculation

8.1 Calculate the modulus of rupture of each specimen as follows:

$$R = 3Wl/2bd^2$$

where:
R = modulus of rupture, psi (or MPa),
W = breaking load, lbf (or N),
l = length of span, in. (or mm),
b = width of specimen, in. (or mm), and
d = thickness of specimen, in. (or mm),

9. Report

9.1 Report the average of all values of modulus of rupture for test specimens loaded perpendicular to the rift as the modulus of rupture perpendicular to the rift, and report the average for all test specimens loaded parallel to the rift as the modulus of rupture parallel to the rift. In case any specimen gives a value of as much as 20 % under the average it shall be examined for defects and, if the low value appears to be due to a flaw or faulty test piece, report the average of the remaining specimens of the group as the modulus of rupture of the sample for the condition of loading under consideration. Report all determinations as information.

9.2 Report the following additional information:

9.2.1 Identification of the sample, including the name and location of the quarry, name and position of the ledge, date when sample was taken, and trade name or grade of the stone,

9.2.2 Size and shape of specimens used in the test, and

9.2.3 A description of the way in which the specimens were prepared.

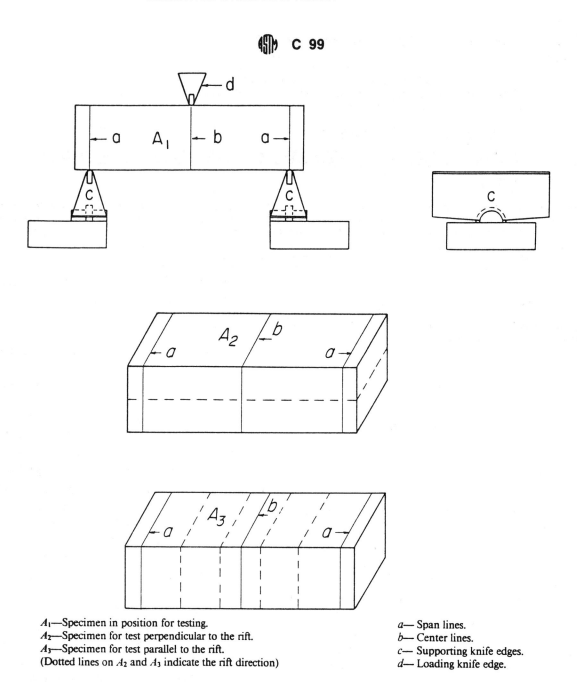

A_1—Specimen in position for testing.
A_2—Specimen for test perpendicular to the rift.
A_3—Specimen for test parallel to the rift.
(Dotted lines on A_2 and A_3 indicate the rift direction)

a— Span lines.
b— Center lines.
c— Supporting knife edges.
d— Loading knife edge.

FIG. 1 Specimens and Preferred Type of Knife Edges for Determining the Modulus of Rupture of Building Stone

Designation: C 170 – 50 (Reapproved 1981)[ε1]

AMERICAN SOCIETY FOR TESTING AND MATERIALS
1916 Race St., Philadelphia, Pa. 19103
Reprinted from the Annual Book of ASTM Standards, Copyright ASTM
If not listed in the current combined index, will appear in the next edition.

Standard Test Method for
COMPRESSIVE STRENGTH OF NATURAL BUILDING STONE[1]

This standard is issued under the fixed designation C 170; the number immediately following the designation indicates the year of original adoption or, in the case of revision, the year of last revision. A number in parentheses indicates the year of last reapproval. A superscript epsilon (ε) indicates an editorial change since the last revision or reapproval.

[ε1] NOTE—Section 2 was added editorially and subsequent sections renumbered in July 1984.

1. Scope

1.1 This test method covers the sampling, preparation of specimens, and determination of the compressive strength of natural building stone.

2. Applicable Document

2.1 *ASTM Standard:*
E 4 Methods of Load Verification of Testing Machines[2]

3. Sampling

3.1 The sample shall be selected to represent a true average of the type or grade of stone under consideration and shall be of the quality supplied to the market in finished form under the type designation to be tested. The sample may be selected by the purchaser or his authorized representative from quarried stone or taken from the natural ledge and shall be of adequate size to permit the preparation of the desired number of test specimens. When perceptible variations occur, the purchaser may select as many samples as are necessary for determining the variation in compressive strength.

4. Apparatus

4.1 Any testing machine conforming to Methods E 4 and to the speed of testing requirements prescribed in Section 7 of this test method may be used.

4.2 In vertical testing machines, the spherical bearing block shall be suspended from the upper head of the machine in such a manner that the contact plate remains in a central position (spherical surfaces in full contact) when not loaded. The spherical surfaces shall be well lubricated, and the center of curvature shall lie in the surface of contact with the specimen.

5. Test Specimens

5.1 The test specimens may be cubes, square prisms, or cylinders and shall be cut from the sample with saws or core drills. The diameter or lateral dimension (distance between opposite vertical faces) shall be not less than 2 in. (50.8 mm) (Note 1), and the ratio of height (Note 2) to diameter or lateral dimension should be not less than 1:1. At least three specimens shall be prepared for each condition of the test; that is, when the compressive strength is desired for the wet and dry conditions but in only one direction, such as perpendicular to the bed (or rift) (see Fig. 1(*a*)), six specimens will be required. For wet and dry strength tests both perpendicular and parallel to the bed (or rift) (see Fig. 1(*a*) and (*b*)), twelve specimens are required (Note 3). The load-bearing faces shall be finished by grinding to as nearly true and parallel planes (Note 4) as practicable.

5.2 The load-bearing surfaces and the direction of bedding (or rift) shall be marked on each specimen after finishing.

5.3 The load-bearing areas of the specimen shall be calculated from measurements taken midway between the load-bearing surfaces. The dimensions of the specimens shall be measured to the nearest 0.02 in. (0.5 mm) and the load-bearing areas calculated to the nearest 0.04 in.^{2} (0.26 cm^2).

[1] This test method is under the jurisdiction of ASTM Committee C-18 on Natural Building Stones and is the direct responsibility of Subcommittee C18.01 on Test Methods.
Current edition approved Sept. 30, 1950. Originally issued 1941. Replaces C 170 – 46.
[2] *Annual Book of ASTM Standards*, Vol 03.01.

6. Conditioning

6.1 *Dry Condition*—Dry specimens to be tested in the dry condition at 221 ± 3.6°F (105 ± 2°C) for 24 h.

6.2 *Wet Condition*—Immerse specimens to be tested in the wet condition in water at 68 ± 9°F (20 ± 5°C) for 48 h and test immediately after removal from the water bath.

7. Procedure

7.1 Center the specimens in the testing machine and apply the initial load at a rate that will permit hand adjustment of the contact plate on the specimen. Rotate the plate back and forth through an angle of about 30° under a small load to properly seat the spherical block, but take care not to move the specimen out of the central position. Preferably, the rate of loading should not exceed 100 psi (690 kPa)/s, but this requirement may be considered as being met if the speed of the loading head is not more than 0.05 in. (1.3 mm)/min.

8. Calculations

8.1 Calculate the compressive strength of each specimen as follows:

$$C = W/A$$

where:

C = compressive strength of the specimen, psi (or MPa)

W = total load, lbf (or N), on the specimen at failure, and

A = calculated area of the bearing surface in in.^{2} (or mm^2).

Round each individual result to the nearest 100 psi (or 1 MPa).

8.2 When the ratio of height to diameter (or lateral dimension) differs from unity by 25 % or more, calculate the result to that of the corresponding cube, as follows:

$$C_c = C_p/[0.778 + 0.222(b + h)]$$

where:

C_c = compressive strength of an equivalent cubical specimen,

C_p = compressive strength of the specimen having a height greater than the diameter or lateral dimension,

b = diameter or lateral dimension, and

h = height.

9. Report

9.1 The average compressive strength of all specimens loaded as shown in Fig. 1(*a*) shall be reported as the compressive strength perpendicular to the bedding (or rift), and the average compressive strength of all specimens loaded as shown in Fig. 1(*b*) shall be reported as the compressive strength parallel to the bedding (or rift).

9.2 The following additional information shall be reported:

9.2.1 Identification of the sample, including name and location of the quarry, name or position of the ledge, date when sample was taken and trade name or grade of stone,

9.2.2 Size and shape of specimens used in the tests, and

9.2.3 A description of the way in which the specimens were prepared.

EXPLANATORY NOTES

NOTE 1—For very coarse-grain materials like some of the granites, the diameter of the specimen should not be less than 2.5 in. (63.5 mm).

NOTE 2—The height of the specimen is considered as the distance between the load-bearing faces.

NOTE 3—In some materials, such as granite, three directions with respect to fissility are recognized, as follows: "rift" (the plane of easiest splitting), "grain" (the plane of next easiest splitting), and "head-grain" (the plane of hardest splitting). Occasionally, tests are required for determining the strength perpendicular to each of these directions. In such cases, the sample shall be marked at the quarry to show which faces are grain, rift, and head-grain, and the required number of specimens shall be prepared with load-bearing faces parallel to each of these planes and properly labeled for the various tests.

NOTE 4—Accuracy of test results depends largely on uniform distribution of the load over the bearing faces. In order to grind the surfaces to reasonably true planes, considerable care is necessary. The following procedure is suggested: Assuming that the specimen is a rectangular prism and the load is to be applied to the ends, mark two adjacent sides for reference, then grind the ends on a grinding wheel or lap until they are perpendicular to these reference sides as gaged by a try square. Complete the grinding by rubbing the ends on a smooth machine-planed surface of a cast iron plate with No. 80 emery and water. The specimen should be grasped as near the surface of the plate as possible to prevent rocking of the specimen. A suitable way to determine when the surfaces are reasonably plane is to dip the specimen in water and press the ends on a smooth machine-planed and polished surface of a 10-lb (4.5-kg) weight. If the weight can be lifted by raising the

⟨ASTM⟩ C 170

specimen, the surfaces may be considered to be sufficiently accurate. A satisfactory mechanical means of finishing the bearing surfaces of the specimens is to place them in a chuck in a lathe and surface the ends with a tool post grinder. This grinder consists of a small motor and arbor carrying an abrasive wheel which turns at about 5000 rpm. A three-point chuck is used to permit the surfacing of cylindrical, square prism, or cubical specimens. When the square-type specimen is used it will be necessary to place a small piece of notched metal between the specimen and one chuck point. This causes the specimen to be placed somewhat off-center but does not interfere with the surfacing process. The surface can be tested for planeness by holding a straightedge on the surface and viewing it before a strong light. Specimens finished in this way commonly give considerably higher test results than specimens prepared by hand.

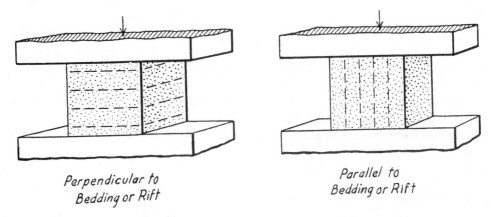

Perpendicular to Bedding or Rift

Parallel to Bedding or Rift

Dashed lines indicate direction of bedding or rift.
Arrows indicate direction of loading.

NOTE—Dashed lines indicate direction of bedding or rift. Arrows indicate direction of loading.

(a) Loading Perpendicular to Bedding or Rift   (b) Loading Parallel to Bedding or Rift

FIG. 1   Methods of Applying Load with Reference to Bedding or Rift

Designation: C 241 – 51 (Reapproved 1981)$^{\epsilon 1}$

AMERICAN SOCIETY FOR TESTING AND MATERIALS
1916 Race St., Philadelphia, Pa. 19103
Reprinted from the Annual Book of ASTM Standards, Copyright ASTM
If not listed in the current combined index, will appear in the next edition.

Standard Test Method for

ABRASION RESISTANCE OF STONE SUBJECTED TO FOOT TRAFFIC[1]

This standard is issued under the fixed designation C 241; the number immediately following the designation indicates the year of original adoption or, in the case of revision, the year of last revision. A number in parentheses indicates the year of last reapproval. A superscript epsilon (ϵ) indicates an editorial change since the last revision or reapproval.

$^{\epsilon 1}$ NOTE—Section 2 was added editorially and subsequent sections renumbered in July 1984.

1. Scope

1.1 This test method covers the determination of the abrasion resistance of all types of stones for floors, steps, and similar uses where the wear is caused by the abrasion of foot traffic.

2. Applicable Document

2.1 *ASTM Standard:*
C 97 Test Methods for Absorption and Bulk Specific Gravity of Natural Building Stone[2]

3. Apparatus

3.1 The abrasion testing apparatus shown in Fig. 1 shall be used. This apparatus consists essentially of a power-driven grinding lap, *A*, 10 in. (254 mm) in diameter, which is revolved at 45 rpm; three specimen holders, *B*, with superimposed weights; gears, *C*, for revolving the specimen; and a means of feeding abrasive at a constant rate to the lap. The guide rings, *D*, are clamped in position slightly above the specimen holders, and the 2000-g weight bearing on the specimen is the combined weight of the specimen holder, vertical shaft above with the attached spur gear, and a weight hopper, *E*, containing additional adjustment weights. The frame, *F*, carrying the guide rings is adjustable vertically to accommodate different specimen thicknesses. Gears, *C*, are adjusted on the shafts for each specimen thickness, so that they are slightly above the plate, *G*, throughout the test.

4. Sampling

4.1 The sample may be selected by the purchaser or his authorized agent but shall represent the average quality of the type or grade of stone under consideration. It shall be of sufficient size to permit the preparation of at least three test specimens, and one face should have the finish to be exposed to traffic. The sample preferably should be 1 in. (25.4 mm) thick and 8 in. (203.2 mm) square.

5. Test Specimens

5.1 At least three specimens 2 in. (50.8 mm) square and preferably 1 in. (25.4 mm) in thickness shall be sawed from the sample. The sharp edges shall be rounded by grinding to a radius of approximately $\frac{1}{32}$ in. (0.8 mm) in order to prevent crumbling during the test.

6. Conditioning

6.1 Dry the test specimens in an oven at 105 ± 2°C for 24 h. If the test is to be made immediately after the specimens have cooled, it is not necessary to place them in a desiccator.

7. Procedure

7.1 Weigh the test specimens to the nearest 0.01 g; then place them in the abrasion testing apparatus and abrade for 225 revolutions of the grinding lap with No. 60 Alundum abrasive (Norton treatment 138S). Remove the specimens from the apparatus, brush them free of dust, and weigh to the same precision as for the original weights.

---

[1] This test method is under the jurisdiction of ASTM Committee C-18 on Natural Building Stones and is the direct responsibility of Subcommittee C18.01 on Test Methods.
Current edition approved Sept. 30, 1951. Originally issued 1950. Replaces C 241 – 50 T.
[2] *Annual Book of ASTM Standards*, Vol 04.08.

C 241

7.2 Place the specimens in water for an hour or more, surface dry them with a towel, and weigh again. Weigh the specimens in water and calculate the bulk specific gravity as described in Test Methods C 97.

NOTE 1—Humidity affects the results to some extent in that the rate of grinding is higher for higher humidity. For this reason it is advisable to make the test when the relative humidity is between 30 and 40 %.

8. Calculation

8.1 Calculate the abrasion resistance of each specimen as follows (Note 2):

$$H_a = 10G(2000 + W_s)/2000 W_a$$

where:
G = bulk specific gravity of the sample,
W_s = average weight of the specimen (original weight plus final weight divided by 2), and

W_a = loss of weight during the grinding operation.

NOTE 2—The abrasive hardness value, H_a, is the reciprocal of the volume of material abraded multiplied by ten. The superimposed weight on the specimen is 2000 g and this is augmented by the weight of the specimen itself. The correction for the weight of the specimen, included in the formula, is based on the fact that the rate of abrasion is directly proportional to the weight. By basing the abrasive resistance values on the volumes, rather than the weights abraded, a better comparison is obtained for materials that vary considerably in bulk density.

9. Report

9.1 The average of the tests on individual specimens, expressed to two significant figures, shall be reported as the abrasive resistance of the sample, but all results shall be reported as information. The report shall identify the type and grade of stone, its source, and the approximate date of removal from the quarry.

C 241

A— Grinding lap.
B— Specimen holders.
C— Gears.
D— Guide rings.

E— Weight hopper.
F— Frame.
G— Plate.

FIG. 1 Apparatus for Abrasion Resistance Test of Stone

ANSI/ASTM C 503 – 79

AMERICAN SOCIETY FOR TESTING AND MATERIALS
1916 Race St., Philadelphia, Pa. 19103
Reprinted from the Annual Book of ASTM Standards, Copyright ASTM
If not listed in the current combined index, will appear in the next edition.

Standard Specification for
MARBLE BUILDING STONE (EXTERIOR)[1]

This standard is issued under the fixed designation C 503; the number immediately following the designation indicates the year of original adoption or, in the case of revision, the year of last revision. A number in parentheses indicates the year of last reapproval.

1. Scope

1.1 This specification covers the material characteristics, physical requirements, and sampling appropriate to the selection of marble for general (exterior) building and structural purposes.

1.2 Building marble shall include stone that is sawed, cut, split, or otherwise finished or shaped, and shall specifically exclude molded, cast, or otherwise artificially aggregated units composed of fragments, and also crushed and broken stone.

2. Applicable Documents

2.1 *ASTM Standards*:
C 97 Test for Absorption and Bulk Specific Gravity of Natural Building Stone[2]
C 99 Test for Modulus of Rupture of Natural Building Stone[2]
C 119 Definitions of Terms Relating to Natural Building Stone[2]
C 170 Test for Compressive Strength of Natural Building Stone[2]
C 241 Test for Abrasion Resistance of Stone Subjected to Foot Traffic[2]

3. Classification

3.1 Building marble (exterior) is classified as follows:

3.1.1 *I Calcite.*
3.1.2 *II Dolomite.*
3.1.3 *III Serpentine.*
3.1.4 *IV Travertine.*

4. Definition

4.1 *marble*—a crystalline rock composed predominantly of one or more of the following minerals: calcite, dolomite, or serpentine and capable of taking a polish (see Definitions C 119).

5. Physical Requirements

5.1 Marble supplied under this specification shall conform to the physical requirements prescribed in Table 1.

5.2 Marble for exterior use shall be sound, free of spalls, cracks, open seams, pits, or other defects that would impair its strength, durability, or appearance.

6. Sampling

6.1 Samples, if required, for testing to determine the characteristics and physical properties shall be representative of the marble to be used.

[1] This specification is under the jurisdiction of ASTM Committee C-18 on Natural Building Stones.
Current edition approved July 27, 1979. Published November 1979. Originally published as C 503 – 62 T. Last previous edition C 503 – 67 (1977).
[2] *Annual Book of ASTM Standards*, Part 19.

⟨ASTM⟩ C 503

TABLE 1 **Physical Requirements**

Physical Property	Test Requirements	Classification	ASTM Test Method
Absorption by weight, max, %	0.75	I, II, III, IV	C 97
Density, min, lb/ft³ (kg/m³):	162 (2595)	I Calcite[A]	C 97
	175 (2800)	II Dolomite[A]	
	168 (2690)	III Serpentine[A]	
	144 (2305)	IV Travertine[A]	
Compressive strength, min, psi(MPa)	7500 (52)	I, II, III, IV	C 170
Modulus of rupture, min, psi(MPa)	1000 (7)	I, II, III, IV	C 99
Abrasion resistance, min, hardness[B]	10	I, II, III, IV	C 241

[A] See Definitions C 119 for definitions of calcite, dolomite, serpentine, and travertine marbles.

[B] Pertains to foot traffic only. Where two or more marbles are combined for color and design effects, there should be no greater difference than 5 points in abrasion resistance. In stairways, floors, and platforms subject to heavy foot traffic, a minimum abrasion hardness of 12.0 is recommended.

ANSI/ASTM C 568 – 79

AMERICAN SOCIETY FOR TESTING AND MATERIALS
1916 Race St., Philadelphia, Pa. 19103
Reprinted from the Annual Book of ASTM Standards, Copyright ASTM
If not listed in the current combined index, will appear in the next edition.

Standard Specification for
LIMESTONE BUILDING STONE[1]

This standard is issued under the fixed designation C 568; the number immediately following the designation indicates the year of original adoption or, in the case of revision, the year of last revision. A number in parentheses indicates the year of last reapproval.

1. Scope

1.1 This specification covers the material characteristics, physical requirements, and sampling appropriate to the selection of limestone for general building and structural purposes.

1.2 Building limestone shall include stone that is sawed, cut, split, or otherwise finished or shaped, and shall specifically exclude molded, cast, or otherwise artificially aggregated units of composed fragments, and also crushed and broken stone.

2. Applicable Documents

2.1 *ASTM Standards*:
C 97 Test for Absorption and Bulk Specific Gravity of Natural Building Stone[2]
C 99 Test for Modulus of Rupture of Natural Building Stone[2]
C 119 Definitions of Terms Relating to Natural Building Stone[2]
C 170 Test for Compressive Strength of Natural Building Stone[2]
C 241 Test for Abrasion Resistance of Stone Subjected to Foot Traffic[2]

3. Classification

3.1 Building limestone may be classified into three categories, generally descriptive of those limestones having densities in approximate ranges, as follows:

3.1.1 *I* (*Low-Density*)—Limestone having a density ranging from 110 through 135 lb/ft^3 (1760 through 2160 kg/m^3).

3.1.2 *II* (*Medium-Density*)—Limestone having a density greater than 135 and not greater than 160 lb/ft^3 (2160 through 2560 kg/m^3).

3.1.3 *III* (*High-Density*)—Limestone having a density greater than 160 lb/ft^3 (2560 kg/m^3).

4. Definition

4.1 *limestone*—a sedimentary rock composed principally of calcium carbonate (the mineral calcite) or the double carbonate of calcium and magnesium (the mineral dolomite) or mixture of the two.

5. Physical Requirements

5.1 Limestone supplied under this specification shall conform to the physical requirements listed in Table 1.

5.2 Limestone shall be sound, durable, and free of visible defects or concentrations of materials that will cause objectionable staining or weakening under normal environments of use.

6. Sampling

6.1 Samples, if required, for testing to determine the characteristics and physical properties shall be representative of the limestone to be used.

---

[1] This specification is under the jurisdiction of ASTM Committee C-18 on National Building Stone.
Current edition approved July 27, 1979. Published November 1979. Originally published as C 568 – 65 T. Last previous edition C 568 – 67 (1977).
[2] *Annual Book of ASTM Standards*, Part 19.

ⒶⓈⓉⓂ C 568

TABLE 1 Physical Requirements

Physical Property	Test Requirements	Classification	ASTM Test Method
Absorption by weight, max, %	12	I low-density	C 97
	7.5	II medium-density	
	3	III high-density	
Density, min, lb/ft^3 (kg/m^3)	110 (1760)	I low-density	C 97
	135 (2160)	II medium-density	
	160 (2560)	III high-density	
Compressive strength, min, psi(MPa)	1800 (12)	I low-density	C 170
	4000 (28)	II medium-density	
	8000 (55)	III high-density	
Modulus of rupture min, psi(MPa)	400 (2.9)	I low-density	C 99
	500 (3.4)	II medium-density	
	1000 (6.9)	III high-density	
Abrasion resistance, min, hardness[A]	10	I low-density	C 241
	10	II medium-density	
	10	III high-density	

[A] Pertains only to stone subject to foot traffic. In stairways, floors, and platforms subject to heavy foot traffic, a minimum abrasion hardness of 10 is recommended.

Designation: C 615 – 80

AMERICAN SOCIETY FOR TESTING AND MATERIALS
1916 Race St., Philadelphia, Pa. 19103
Reprinted from the Annual Book of ASTM Standards, Copyright ASTM
If not listed in the current combined index, will appear in the next edition.

Standard Specification for
GRANITE BUILDING STONE[1]

This standard is issued under the fixed designation C 615; the number immediately following the designation indicates the year of original adoption or, in the case of revision, the year of last revision. A number in parentheses indicates the year of last reapproval.

1. Scope

1.1 This specification covers the material characteristics, physical requirements, and sampling appropriate to the selection of granite for general building and structural purposes.

1.2 Building granite shall include stone that is sawed, cut, split, or otherwise finished or shaped, and shall specifically exclude molded, cast, or otherwise artificially aggregated units composed of fragments, and also crushed and broken stone.

2. Applicable Documents

2.1 *ASTM Standards*:
C 97 Tests for Absorption and Bulk Specific Gravity of Natural Building Stone[2]
C 99 Test for Modulus of Rupture of Natural Building Stone[2]
C 119 Definitions of Terms Relating to Natural Building Stone[2]
C 170 Test for Compressive Strength of Natural Building Stone[2]
C 241 Test for Abrasion Resistance of Stone Subjected to Foot Traffic[2]

3. Classification

3.1 Building granite under this specification shall be granite used for:
Bridge piers, sea and river walls, dams, and related structures;
Bridge superstructures, grade separations, and retaining walls;
Flexural members;
Curbstone and pavements;
Monumental structures;
Institutional, commercial, and residential buildings, and landscaping, parks, and other ornamental improvements.

4. Physical Requirements

4.1 Granite supplied under this specification shall conform to the physical requirements prescribed in Table 1.

4.2 Granite shall be sound, durable, and free of imperfections such as starts, cracks, and seams that would impair its structural integrity.

4.3 Granite shall be free of minerals that may cause objectionable staining under normal environments of use.

4.4 The desired color and the permissible natural variations in color and texture shall be specified by carefully detailed description or naming granite having the required characteristics.

5. Sampling

5.1 Samples, if required, for testing to determine the characteristics and physical properties shall be representative of the granite to be used.

---

[1] This specification is under the jurisdiction of ASTM Committee C-18 on Natural Building Stones and is the direct responsibility of Subcommittee C18.03 on Material Specifications.
Current edition approved April 25, 1980. Published June 1980. Originally published as C 615 – 68. Last previous edition C 615 – 68 (1977).
[2] *Annual Book of ASTM Standards*, Part 19.

C 615

TABLE 1 Physical Requirements

Physical Property	Test Requirements	ASTM Test Method
Absorption by weight, max, %	0.4	C 97
Density, min, lb/ft³ (kg/m³)	160 (2560)	C 97
Compressive strength, min, psi (MPa)	19 000 (131)	C 170
Modulus of rupture, min, psi (MPa)	1500 (10.34)	C 99
Abrasion resistance, min H_a	[A]	C 241

[A] The minimum H_a value has not been established at this time and is presently a topic of study by Committee C-18.

ANSI/ASTM C 616 – 80

AMERICAN SOCIETY FOR TESTING AND MATERIALS
1916 Race St., Philadelphia, Pa. 19103
Reprinted from the Annual Book of ASTM Standards, Copyright ASTM
If not listed in the current combined index, will appear in the next edition.

Standard Specification for
SANDSTONE BUILDING STONE[1]

This standard is issued under the fixed designation C 616; the number immediately following the designation indicates the year of original adoption or, in the case of revision, the year of last revision. A number in parentheses indicates the year of last reapproval.

1. Scope

1.1 This specification covers the material characteristics, physical requirements, and sampling appropriate to the selection of sandstone for general building and structural purposes.

1.2 Building sandstone shall include stone that is sawed, cut, split, or otherwise finished or shaped, and shall specifically exclude molded, cast, or otherwise artifically aggregated units composed of fragments, and also crushed and broken stone.

2. Applicable Documents

2.1 *ASTM Standards*:
C 97 Test for Absorption and Bulk Specific Gravity of Natural Building Stone[2]
C 99 Test for Modulus of Rupture of Natural Building Stone[2]
C 119 Definitions of Terms Relating to Natural Building Stones[2]
C 170 Test for Compressive Strength of Natural Building Stone[2]
C 241 Test for Abrasion Resistance of Stone Subjected to Foot Traffic[2]

3. Classification

3.1 Building sandstone shall be classified according to the free silica content as follows:

3.1.1 *I Sandstone*, with 60 % minimum free silica content.[3]

3.1.2 *II Quartzitic Sandstone*, with 90 % minimum free silica content.

3.1.3 *III Quartzite*, with 95 % minimum free silica content.

4. Physical Requirements

4.1 Sandstone supplied under this specification shall conform to the physical requirements in Table 1.

5. Sampling

5.1 Samples, if required, for testing to determine the characteristics and physical properties shall be representative of the sandstone to be used.

---

[1] This specification is under the jurisdiction of ASTM Committee C-18 on Natural Building Stones.
   Current edition approved Jan. 25, 1980. Published March 1980. Originally published as C 616 – 68. Last previous edition C 616 – 68 (1977).
[2] *Annual Book of ASTM Standards*, Part 19.
[3] Free silica consists of detrital quartz grains plus authigenic silica.

ASTM C 616

TABLE 1 Physical Requirements

Property	Test Requirements	Classifications	ASTM Test Method
Absorption by weight, max, %	20	I Sandstone	C 97
	3	II Quartzitic Sandstone	
	1	III Quartzite	
Density, min, lb/ft^3 (kg/m^3)	140 (2240)	I Sandstone	C 97
	150 (2400)	II Quartzitic Sandstone	
	160 (2560)	III Quartzite	
Compressive strength, min, psi (MPa)	2000 (13.8)	I Sandstone	C 170
	10000 (68.9)	II Quartzitic Sandstone	
	20000 (137.9)	III Quartzite	
Modulus of rupture, min, psi (MPa)	300 (2.1)	I Sandstone	C 99
	1000 (6.9)	II Quartzitic Sandstone	
	2000 (13.9)	III Quartzite	
Abrasion resistance	8	I Sandstone	C 241
	8	II Quartzitic Sandstone	
	8	III Quartzite	

ANSI/ASTM C 629 – 80

AMERICAN SOCIETY FOR TESTING AND MATERIALS
1916 Race St., Philadelphia, Pa. 19103
Reprinted from the Annual Book of ASTM Standards, Copyright ASTM
If not listed in the current combined index, will appear in the next edition.

Standard Specification for
SLATE BUILDING STONE[1]

This standard is issued under the fixed designation C 629; the number immediately following the designation indicates the year of original adoption or, in the case of revision, the year of last revision. A number in parentheses indicates the year of last reapproval.

1. Scope

1.1 This specification covers the material characteristics, physical requirements, and sampling appropriate to the selection of slate for general building and structural purposes.

1.2 Building slate shall include stone that is sawed, cut, split, or otherwise finished or shaped, and shall specifically exclude molded, cast, or otherwise artificially aggregated units composed of fragments, and also crushed and broken stone.

1.3 It specifically excludes roofing slate (see ASTM Specification C 406, for Roofing Slate), blackboard slate (see ASTM Specification C 543, for Slate Blackboards), and slate for industrial uses.

2. Applicable Documents

2.1 *ASTM Standards*:
C 119 Definitions of Terms Relating to Natural Building Stones[2]
C 120 Flexure Testing of Slate (Modulus of Rupture, Modulus of Elasticity)[2]
C 121 Test for Water Absorption of Slate[2]
C 217 Test for Weather Resistance of Natural Slate[2]
C 241 Test for Abrasion Resistance of Stone Subjected to Foot Traffic[2]

3. Classification

3.1 Building slate shall be selected for the following uses:
3.1.1 *I Exterior*.
3.1.2 *II Interior*.

4. Physical Requirements

4.1 Slate supplied under this specification shall conform to the requirements listed in Table 1.

4.2 Slate used for exterior applications in ambient acidic atmospheres or in industrial areas where heavy air pollution occurs shall be free of carbonaceous ribbons.

4.3 Slate shall be selected for overall satisfactory and natural appearance.

4.4 Slate shall be sound, free of spalls, pits, cracks, or other defects that would impair its strength or durability.

5. Sampling

5.1 Samples, if required, for testing to determine the characteristics and physical properties shall be representative of the slate to be used.

---

[1] This specification is under the jurisdiction of ASTM Committee C-18 on Natural Building Stones.
Current edition approved Jan. 25, 1980. Published March 1980. Originally published as C 629 – 68. Last previous edition C 629 – 68 (1977).
[2] *Annual Book of ASTM Standards*, Part 19.

C 629

TABLE 1 Physical Requirements

Property	Test Requirements	Classifications	ASTM Test Methods
Absorption, max, %	0.25	I Exterior	C 121
	0.45	II Interior	
Modulus of rupture, min, psi (MPa):			
Across grain	9000 (62.1)	I Exterior	C 120
	9000 (62.1)	II Interior	
Along grain	7200 (49.6)	I Exterior	
	7200 (49.6)	II Interior	
Abrasion resistance	8.0	I Exterior	C 241
	8.0	II Interior	
Acid resistance, max, in. (mm)	0.015 (0.38)	I Exterior	C 217
	0.025 (0.64)	II Interior	

Designation: C 880 – 89

AMERICAN SOCIETY FOR TESTING AND MATERIALS
1916 Race St., Philadelphia, Pa. 19103
Reprinted from the Annual Book of ASTM Standards, Copyright ASTM
If not listed in the current combined index, will appear in the next edition.

Standard Test Method for
Flexural Strength of Natural Building Stone[1]

This standard is issued under the fixed designation C 880; the number immediately following the designation indicates the year of original adoption or, in the case of revision, the year of last revision. A number in parentheses indicates the year of last reapproval. A superscript epsilon (ε) indicates an editorial change since the last revision or reapproval.

[1] NOTE—The equation in 9.1.6 was changed editorially on Jan. 9, 1989.

1. Scope

1.1 This test method covers the procedure for determining the flexural strength of stone by use of a simple beam using quarter-point loading.

1.2 Stone tests shall be made when pertinent for the situation when the load is perpendicular to the bedding plane and when the load is parallel to the bedding plane.

1.3 As required, the flexural tests shall also be conducted under wet conditions.

1.4 The values stated in SI units are to be regarded as the standard.

1.5 *This standard may involve hazardous materials, operations, and equipment. This standard does not purport to address all of the safety problems associated with its use. It is the responsibility of the user of this standard to establish appropriate safety and health practices and determine the applicability of regulatory limitations prior to use.*

2. Referenced Document

2.1 *ASTM Standard:*
E 4 Practices for Load Verification of Testing Machines[2]

3. Significance and Use

3.1 This test method is useful in indicating the differences in flexural strength between the various building stones. This test method also provides one element in comparing stones of the same type.

4. Apparatus

4.1 *Testing Machine* (Fig. 1), conforming to the requirements of the applicable sections of Practices E 4. The quarter-point loading method shall be used in making flexure tests of stone employing bearing blocks which will ensure that forces applied to the beam will be vertical only and applied without eccentricity. The apparatus should be capable of maintaining the span length and distances between load-applying blocks and support blocks constant within ±1.3 mm (±0.05 in.). The load should be capable of being applied at a uniform rate and in such a manner as to avoid shock.

5. Test Specimens

5.1 The test specimens shall have a span as nearly as practicable 10 times its depth as tested and a width 1.5 times its depth. The minimum depth of the specimen shall be 25 mm (1 in.). A recommended specimen size is 38 mm (1½ in.) wide by 25 mm (1 in.) thick by 300 mm (12 in.) long. The sides of the specimen shall be at right angles with the top and bottom. The specimens shall have a fine abrasive finish on the planes perpendicular to the load and a fine saw finish on the other four planes. The dimensions of the specimen shall be measured and recorded to the nearest 0.3 mm (0.01 in.). A minimum of five specimens shall be tested.

5.2 Test results obtained by this test method are those of flexural strength properties. In specific applications, test specimens of different geometry may give useful results in terms of a modulus of rupture value.

6. Conditioning

6.1 Before testing the specimens in a dry condition, dry them for 48 h at 60 ± 2°C (156 ± 4°F). At the 46th, 47th and 48th hour, weigh the specimens to ensure that the weight is the same. If the weight continues to drop, continue to dry the specimens until there are three successive hourly readings with the same weight. After removing the specimens from the oven, cool them to room temperature in a desiccator before testing them.

6.2 Before testing the specimens in a wet condition, immerse them in water for 48 h at 22 ± 2°C (72 ± 4°F). Test them immediately upon removal from the bath, wiping the specimens free of surface water.

7. Procedure

7.1 Assemble the apparatus and place the specimen on the span supports and adjust the quarter point loading blocks into contact with the specimen.

7.2 Then increase the load at 535 N/min (120 lbf/min), which corresponds to a stress rate of 4.14 MPa (600 psi)/min, a deflection rate of 0.015 mm (0.0006 in.)/min, and a crosshead movement of 0.6 mm (0.025 in.)/min. Apply the load to failure at a rate of 69 kPa (10 psi)/s.

8. Calculation

8.1 Calculate the flexural strength, σ, as follows:

$$\sigma = \frac{3}{4}\frac{WL}{bd^2}$$

where:
σ = flexural strength, MPa (psi),

---

[1] This test method is under the jurisdiction of ASTM Committee C-18 on Natural Building Stones and is the direct responsibility of Subcommittee C18.01 on Test Methods.
Current edition approved Jan. 9, 1989. Published February 1989. Originally published as C 880 – 78. Last previous edition C 880 – 87.
[2] *Annual Book of ASTM Standards*, Vol 03.01.

C 880

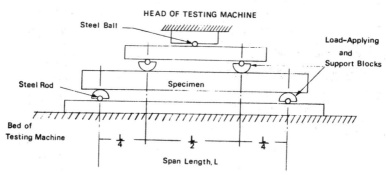

NOTE—Apparatus may be used inverted.

FIG. 1   Diagrammatic View of a Suitable Apparatus for Flexure Test of Stone

W = maximum load, N (lbf),
L = span, mm (in.); $L = 10d$,
b = width of specimen, mm (in.); $b = 1.5d$, and
d = depth of specimen, mm (in.).

9. Report

9.1 The report shall include the following:

9.1.1 Stone type.

9.1.2 Sizes of the specimens used.

9.1.3 Preconditioning procedure used.

9.1.4 Individual test results for each specimen.

9.1.5 Average value of the test results for each group using the following relation:

$$\overline{\sigma} = \frac{\text{sum of observed values}}{\text{number of tests}}$$

9.1.6 Standard deviation, s, of the test results for each group using the following relation:

$$s = \sqrt{\frac{\text{sum of (observed value} - \overline{\sigma})^2}{\text{number of tests} - 1}}$$

9.1.7 Any variations from the above procedural techniques.

10. Precision and Bias

10.1 Individual variations in a natural product may result in deviation from accepted values. A precision section will be added when sufficient data are available to indicate acceptable tolerances in repeatability and reproducibility.

9
Glossary of Stone Terms

A

ABRASIVE FINISH—A finish applied to fabricated stones that gives an even non-reflective surface.

ABUTMENT—A solid stone ''springer'' at the lowest point of an arch or vault.

ADHERED—Veneer secured and supported through adhesion to an approved bonding material applied over an approved backing.

AGATE—A variegated variety of quartz showing colored bands or other markings (clouded, moss-like, etc.).

ANCHORS—Types for stonework include those made of flat stock (strap, cramps, dovetails, dowel, strap and dowel, and two-way anchors) and round stock (rod cramp, rod anchor, eyebolt and dowel, flat-hood wall tie and dowel, dowel and wire toggle bolts).

Figure 9-1
Strap anchor with drop dowel in sandstone anchored to concrete.

115

ARCH—A curved stone structure resting on supports at both extremities used to sustain weight, to bridge or roof an open space.

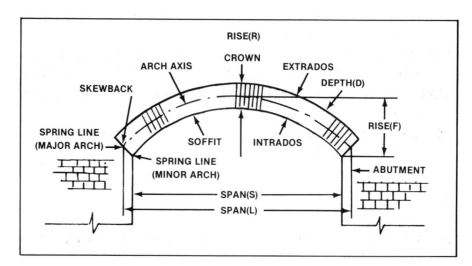

Figure 9-2
Arch terminology.

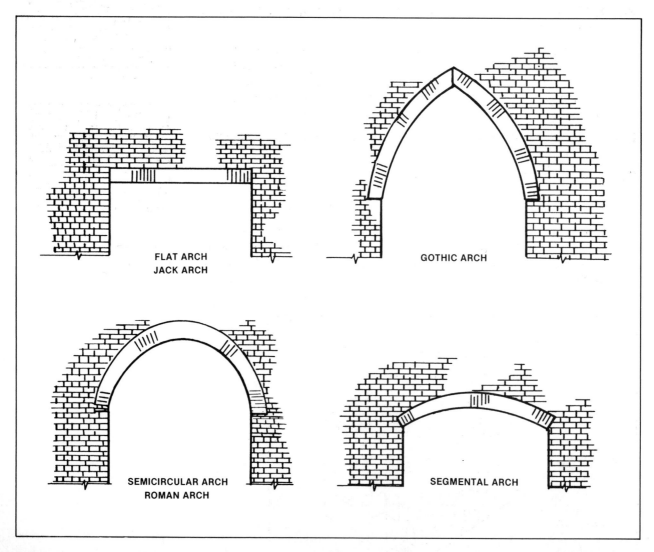

Figure 9-3
Types of arches.

ARCHITRAVE—The member of an entablature resting on the capitals of columns and supporting the frieze.

ARGILLITE—A compact sedimentary rock composed mainly of clay and aluminum silicate minerals.

ARKOSE—A sandstone containing 10 percent or more clastic grains of feldspar. Also called ARKOSIC SANDSTONE, FELDSPATHIC SANDSTONE.

ARRIS—A natural or applied line on the stone from which all leveling and plumbing is measured.

ASHLAR—Masonry having a face of square or rectangular stones, either smooth or textured.

B

BACK ARCH—A concealed arch carrying the backing of a wall where the exterior facing is carried by a lintel.

BALUSTER—A miniature pillar or column supporting a rail; used in balustrades.

BASALT—A dense-textured (aphanitic), igneous rock relatively high in iron and magnesia minerals and relatively low in silica, generally dark gray to black, and feldspathic. A general term in contradistinction to felsite, a light-colored feldspathic and highly siliceous rock of similar texture and origin.

BED—The top or bottom of a joint, natural bed; surface of stone parallel to its stratification.

BED—(1) In granites and marbles, a layer or sheet of the rock mass that is horizontal, commonly curved and lenticular, as developed by fractures. Sometimes applied also to the surface of parting between sheets.

(2) In stratified rocks the unit layer formed by semidentation; of variable thickness, and commonly tilted or distorted by subsequent deformation; generally develops a rock cleavage, parting, or jointing along the planes of stratification.

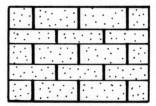
RANGE COURSE

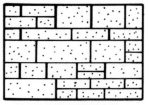
BROKEN RANGE

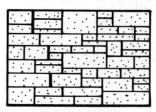
RANDOM RANGE

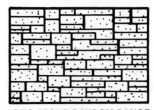
LONG STONE RANDOM RANGE

Figure 9-4
Ashlar masonry.

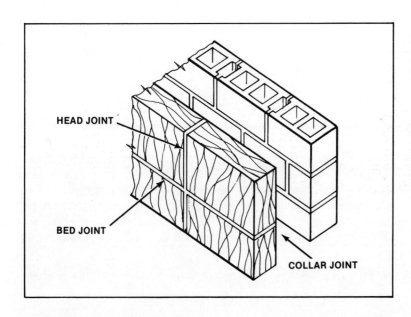

HEAD JOINT

BED JOINT

COLLAR JOINT

Figure 9-5
Bed, head, and collar joints.

BELT COURSE—A continuous horizontal course of flat stones placed in line marking a division in the wall plane.

BEVEL—When the angle between two sides is greater or less than a right angle.

BLUESTONE—A dense, hard, fine-grained, commonly feldspathic sandstone or siltstone of medium to dark or bluish-gray color that splits readily along original bedding planes to form thin slabs. Bluestone is not a technical geologic term. It is considered to be a variety of flagstone, the thin, relatively smooth-surfaced slabs being suitable for use as flagging. The term has been applied particularly to sandstones of Devonian age that are being or have been quarried in eastern New York and Pennsylvania and in western New Jersey, but similar stones that occur elsewhere may be included. It has also been applied in places to thinly-layered gneisses and schists that can be split and used as flagging, but such stones are not properly embraced by this definition, although they may be marketed properly as flagstone.

BOND STONE—Used in varying percentages to anchor or bond the stone veneer to the backing material. Bond stones are generally cut to twice the bed thickness of the material being used.

BORDER STONE—Usually a flat stone used as an edging material. A border stone is generally used to retain the field of the terrace or platform.

BOX—A tapered metal box wedged in the top of columns or other heavy stones for hoisting.

BROACH—(1) To drill or cut out material left between closely spaced drill holes.
(2) A mason's sharp-pointed chisel for dressing stone.
(3) An inclined piece of masonry filling the triangular space between the base of an octagonal spire and the top of a square tower.
(4) A type of chisel used for working narrow surfaces.

BROWNSTONE—A sandstone of characteristic brown or reddish-brown color that is due to a prominent amount of iron oxide, as interstitial material.

BRUSHED FINISH—Obtained by brushing the stone with a coarse rotary-type wire brush.

BUILDING STONE, NATURAL—Rock material in its natural state of composition and aggregation as it exists in the quarry and is usable in construction as dimension building stone.

BULL NOSE—Convex rounding of a stone member, such as a stair tread.

C

CALCARENITE—Limestone composed predominantly of clastic sand-size grains of calcite, or rarely aragonite, usually as fragments of shells or other skeletal structures. Some calcarenites contain oolites (small, spherical grains of calcium carbonate that resemble roe) and may be termed oolite limestone. Calcareous sandstones, in which the calcium carbonate is present chiefly as bonding material, are not included in this category.

CALCITE LIMESTONE—A limestone containing not more than five percent of magnesium carbonate.

CALCITE STREAKS—Description of a white or milky-like streak occurring in stone. It is a joint plane usually wider than a glass seam and has been recemented by deposition of calcite in the crack and is structurally sound.

CANOPY—A sheltering roof, as over a niche or a doorway.

CAPITAL—The culminating stone at the top of a column or pilaster, often richly carved.

CARVE—Shaping, by cutting a design to form the trade of a sculptor.

CAULKING—Making a marble joint tight or leak-proof by sealing with an elastic adhesive compound.

CAVITY VENT—A vent or opening in the joints between stones to provide even atmospheric pressure and humidity between the cavity and outside air; to prevent condensation and the migration of water into the structure.

CEMENT PUTTY—A thick, creamy mixture made with pure cement and water which is used to strengthen the bond between the stone and the setting bed. Also called CEMENT BUTTER, CEMENT CREAM.

CHAMFER—To bevel the junction of an exterior angle.

CHAT-SAWN FINISH—A rough gang saw finish produced by sawing with coarse chat.

CLADDING—Non-load-bearing thin stone slabs used for facing buildings.

CLEAVAGE—The ability of a rock mass to break along natural surfaces; a surface of natural parting.

CLEAVAGE PLANE—Plane or planes along which a stone may likely break or delaminate.

COATING—A protective or decorative covering applied to the surface or impregnated into stone for such purposes as waterproofing, enhancing resistance to weathering, wear, and chemical action, or improving appearance of the stone.

COBBLESTONE—A natural rounded stone, large enough for use in paving. Commonly used to describe paving blocks, usually granite, generally cut to rectangular shapes.

COMMERCIAL MARBLE—A crystalline rock composed predominantly of one or more of the following materials: calcite dolomite or serpentine, and capable of taking a polish.

COMPOSITE—A construction unit in which stone that is to be exposed in the final use is permanently bonded or joined to other material, which may be stone or manufactured material, that will be concealed.

CONTRACTION JOINTS—Spaces where panels are joined and which expand as the panels contract.

CONTROL JOINT—Provided so that the movement of different parts of the structure due to shrinkage, expansion, temperature changes or other causes do not transfer loads across the joint.

COPING—A flat stone used as a cap on free-standing walls.

COQUINA—A limestone composed predominantly of unaltered shells or fragments of shells loosely cemented by calcite. Coquina is generally very coarse-textured and has a high porosity. The term has been applied principally to a very porous shell rock of Eocene age that has been quarried in Florida.

CORBEL PLATES—Plates of non-ferrous metal fixed into a structure to support stone cladding at intervals and over openings in such a way as not to be visible.

CORNERSTONE—A stone forming a part of a corner or angle in a wall. Also a stone laid at the formal inauguration of the erection of a building, not necessarily at a corner, usually incorporating a date or inscription.

CORNICE—A molded projecting stone at the top or an entablature.

COURSE—A horizontal range of stone units the length of the wall.

COURSED VENEER—This is achieved by using stones of the same or approximately the same heights. Horizontal joints run the entire length of the veneered area. Vertical joints are constantly broken so that no two joints will be over one another.

CROSS-BEDDING—The arrangement of laminations of strata transverse or oblique to the main planes of stratification.

CROWFOOT (STYOLITE)—Description of a dark gray to black zigzag marking occurring in stone. Usually structurally sound.

CRYSTALLINE LIMESTONE—A limestone, either calcitic or dolomitic, composed of interlocking crystalline grains of the constituent minerals and of phaneritic texture. Commonly used synonymously with marble and thus representing a re-crystallized limestone. Improperly applied to limestones that display some obviously crystalline grains in a fine-grained mass but which are not of interlocking texture and do not compose the entire mass. (NOTE: All limestones are microscopically, or in part megascopically, crystalline; the term is thus confusing, but should be restricted to stones that are completely crystalline and of megascopic and interlocking texture and that may be classed as marbles.)

CURBING—Slabs and blocks of stone bordering streets, walks, etc.

CUT STONE—This includes all stone cut or machined to give sizes, dimension or shape, and produced in accordance with working or shop drawings which have been developed from the architect's structural drawings.

CUTTING STOCK—A term used to describe slabs of varying size, finish, and thickness which are used in fabricating treads, risers, copings, borders, sills, stools, hearths, mantels, and other special purpose stones.

D

DACITE—A fine-grained, extrusive (volcanic) rock, intermediate in color and composition between basalt and rhyolite.

DAMP-PROOFING—One or more coatings of a compound that is impervious to water applied to a surface above grade.

DENTIL—Block projections on an entablature.

DENTIL COURSE—The lower part of the cornice with dentils. The cornice is jointed to allow machine production of the dentils.

DENTILS—Small, rectangular blocks under a classical cornice, resembling a row of teeth.

DIMENSION STONE—Quarried stones, generally two feet or more square, of a specified thickness. Usually with one or more mechanically dressed surfaces.

DOLOMITIC LIMESTONE—A limestone rich in magnesium carbonate, frequently somewhat crystalline in character. It is found in ledge formations in a wide variety of color tones and textures. Generally speaking, its crushing and tensile strengths are greater than the oolitic limestones and its appearance shows greater variety in texture.

DOWEL—A short piece of non-ferrous metal or slate fixed into a mortice or sinking in the joints of adjoining stones to prevent movement.

DRESSED or HAND-DRESSED—The cutting of rough chunks of stone by hand to create a square or rectangular shape. A stone which is sold as dressed stone generally refers to stone ready for installation. Sometimes called scabbling.

DRIP—A recess cut beneath and slightly behind projecting stone to prevent water from running down the face of the wall below.

DRIPSTONE—A projecting moulding over the heads of doorways, windows and archways to throw off the rain. Also known as a "hoodmould" and, when rectangular, as a "label."

DRY—An open or unhealed joint plane not filled with calcite and not structurally sound.

DRY WALL—A dry wall is a stone wall that is constructed one stone upon the other without the use of any mortar. Generally used for retaining walls.

DURABILITY—The measure of the ability of natural building stone to endure and to maintain its essential and distinctive characteristics of strength, resistance to decay, and appearance, with relation to a specific manner, purpose, and environment of use.

E

EFFLORESCENCE—A crystalline deposit appearing on stone surfaces typically caused by soluble salts carried through or onto the stone by moisture, which has sometimes been found to come from brick, tile, concrete blocks, cement, mortar, concrete, and similar materials in the wall or above.

ENTABLATURE—In classical architecture, the upper part of an order, comprising architrave, frieze, and cornice.

ENTASIS—The curve of the upper two-thirds of a column.

EXPANSION BOLT—A socket that grips a drilled hole in stone by expanding as the bolt is screwed into it.

EXPANSION-CONTRACTION JOINT—A joint in a wall designed to allow the expansion and contraction of the wall due to temperature change. An expansion joint compresses as panels expand, a contraction joint expands as panels contract.

EXPOSED AGGREGATE—Phrase applied to the larger pieces of stone aggregate purposefully exposed for their color and texture in a cast slab.

F

FACE—This refers to the exposed portion of stone. The word "face" can also be used when referring to the edge treatment on various cutting stock materials.

FASCIA—A horizontal belt or vertical face; often used in combination with moldings.

FERRUGINOUS—Limestone or sandstone containing a high proportion of iron oxide.

FIELD STONE—Loose blocks separated from ledges by natural processes and scattered through or upon the regolith ("soil") cover; applied also to similar transported materials, such as glacial boulders and cobbles.

FILLING—Filling the natural voids and veins in a stone with material (cement, shellac, or synthetic resins and similar materials often mixed with stone fines).

FINES—The residue resulting from the normal fabrication and processing of stone.

FINISH—The final appearance exposed stone slab surfaces are fabricated to meet.

FIREPROOF—Relatively incombustible.

FLAGSTONE—Thin slabs of stone used for flagging or paving walks, driveways, patios, etc. It is generally fine-grained sandstone, bluestone, quartzite or slate, but thin slabs of other stones may be used.

FLEURI CUT—Cutting quarried marble or stone parallel to the natural bedding plane.

FREESTONE—A stone that may be cut freely in any direction without fracture or splitting.

FRIEZE—A belt course, sometimes decorated with sculpture relief, occurring just under a cornice.

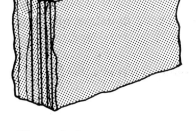

Figure 9-6
Fleuri cut.

G

GANG SAWED—Description of the granular surface of stone resulting from gang sawing alone.

GAUGED or GAUGING—A grinding process to make all pieces of material to be used together the same thickness.

GLASS SEAM—Description of a narrow glass-like streak occurring in stone. It is a joint plane that has been recemented by deposition of translucent calcite in the crack and is structurally sound.

GRADE COURSE—Beginning course at the grade level, generally waterproofed with a dampcheck or damp course.

GRAIN—The easiest cleavage direction in a stone. "With the grain" same as "natural bed." Also, particles (crystals, sand grains, etc.) or a rock.

GRANITE—A fine to coarse-grained, igneous rock formed by volcanic action consisting of quartz, feldspar, and mica, with accessory minerals. Granite-type rocks include those of similar texture and origin.

GRANITE (scientific definition)—A visibly granular, crystalline rock of predominantly interlocking texture, composed essentially of alkalic feldspars and quartz; this is true granite. Feldspar is generally present in excess of quartz, and accessory minerals (chiefly micas, hornblende, or more rarely pyroxene) are commonly present. The alkalic feldspars may be present (1) as individual mineral species, (2) as isomorphous or mechanical intergrowths with each other, or (3) as chemical intergrowths with the lime feldspar molecule, but 80 + 3 percent of the feldspar must be composed of the potash or soda feldspar molecules.

GRANITE (commercial/building use)—A term that includes granite (as defined above), gneiss, gneissic granite, granite gneiss, and the rock species known to petrologists as syenite, monzonite, and granodiorite, species intermediate between them, the gneissic varieties and gneisses of corresponding mineralogic compositions and the corresponding varieties of porphyritic textures. The term commercial granite shall also include other feldspathic crystalline rocks of similar textures, containing minor amounts of accessory minerals, used for special decorative purposes, and known to petrologists as anorthosite and laurvikite,

GRANITE GNEISS—A foliated crystalline rock composed essentially of silicate minerals with interlocking and visibly granular texture, and in which the foliation is due primarily to alternating layers, regular or irregular, of contrasting mineralogic composition. In general, a gneiss is characterized by relatively thick layers as compared with a schist. According to their mineralogic compositions, gneisses may correspond to other rocks of crystalline, visibly granular, interlocking texture, such as those included under the definition of commercial granite, and may then be known as granitegneiss if strongly foliated, or gneissic granite if weakly foliated.

BLACK GRANITE—Rock species known to petrologists as diabase, diorite, gabbro, and intermediate varieties are sometimes quarried as building stone, chiefly for ornamental use, and sold as "black granite." As dimension blocks or slabs, they are valued specifically for their dark gray to black color when polished. Scientifically, they are far removed in composition from true granites though they may be satisfactorily used for some of the purposes to which commercial granites are adapted. They possess an interlocking crystalline texture, but unlike granites, they contain little or no quartz or alkalic feldspar, and are characterized by an abundance of one or more of the common black rock-forming minerals (chiefly pyroxenes, hornblende, and biotite).

GREENSTONE—Includes stones that have been metamorphosed or otherwise changed that they have assumed a distinctive greenish color owing to the presence of one or more of the following minerals: chlorite, epidote, or actinolite.

GROUT—Pourable cementitious material. COARSE GROUT, used for wide grout spaces 2'' or more, consists of one part Portland cement, two-and-a-quarter to three parts sand, and one to two parts pea gravel. FINE GROUT, used in narrow grout spaces, consists of one part Portland cement and two-and-a-quarter to three parts sand.

H

HAND-CUT RANDOM RECTANGULAR ASHLAR—A pattern where all the stone is hand cut into squares and rectangulars. Joints are fairly consistent. Similar to sawed-bed ashlar in appearance.

HAND or MACHINE PITCH-FACED (ROCK-FACED) ASHLAR—A finish given to both veneer stone and cutting stock. This is created by establishing a straight line back from the irregular face of the stone. Proper tools are then used to cut along the line, leaving a straight arris and the intended rustic finish on the face.

HEAD—The end of a stone which has been tooled to match the face of the stone. Heads are used at outside corners, windows, door jambs, or any place where the veneering will be visible from the side.

HEARTH—That part of the floor of a fireplace of stone on which the fire is laid.

HEARTH STONE—Origianlly the single large stone or stones used for the hearth, now most commonly used to describe the stone in front of the fire chamber and many times extending on either or both sides of the front of the fire chamber.

HOLES—Sinkages in the top beds of stones to engage Lewis pins for hoisting.

HONED FINISH—Honed is a super-fine smooth finish, though not as fine as a polished finish.

I

IGNEOUS—One of the three great classes of rock (igneous, sedimentary and metamorphic), solidified from molten state, as granite and lavas.

INCISE—To cut inwardly or engrave, as in an inscription.

INSCRIPTION—Lettering cut in stone.

J

JACK ARCH—One having horizontal or nearly horizontal upper and lower surfaces. Also called flat or straight arch.

JOINT—The space between stone units, usually filled with mortar. Types of joints are shown in Figure 9–7.

JOINTING SCHEME—A detailed architectural drawing showing the dimensions, locations and configurations of stone units and joints on the structure.

JUMPER—In ashlar patterns, a piece of stone of higher rise than adjacent stones which is used to end a horizontal mortar joint at the point where it is set.

K

KEYSTONE—The last wedge-shaped stone placed in the crown of an arch regarded as binding the whole.

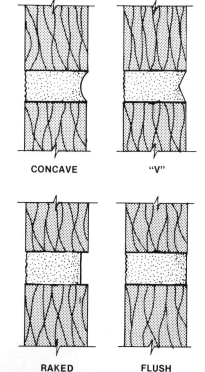

CONCAVE   "V"

RAKED   FLUSH

Figure 9–7
Joints.

L

LAVA—A general term applied to igneous rocks, such as basalt and rhyolite, that erupted from the earth by volcanic action.

LEAD BUTTONS—Lead spacers in the solid horizontal joints to support the top stones until the mortar has set.

LEWIS HOLES—Holes in cut stones for lifting and support during setting of cut stones and sometimes for permanent support. Holes are checked for the particular Lewis lifting device or hook to be used.

LIMESTONE—A sedimentary rock composed of calcium carbonate; includes many varieties. (See oolitic limestone, dolomitic limestone, crystalline limestone.) Limestones that contain not more than five percent magnesium carbonate may be termed calcite limestone, as distinguished from those that contain between five and 40 percent magnesium carbonate (magnesium or dolomitic limestone), and from those that contain in excess of 40 percent as the mineral dolomite (dolostone, formerly known as the rock dolomite). Recrystalized limestones and compact, dense, relatively pure microcrystaline varities that are capable of taking a polish are included in commercial marbles.

LINERS—Strengthening elements attached to the back of stone slabs, usually a structurally sound section of similar stone dowelled and epoxied into place.

LINTEL—The block of stone spanning the top of an opening such as a doorway or window; sometimes called a head.

LIPPING—Usually refers to flagging materials. Lipping is caused when two pieces of material to be joined together are slightly warped or twisted causing one or more edges to be higher or lower than the adjoining material.

LUG SILL—A stone sill set into the jambs on each side of masonry opening.

M

MACHINE FINISH—The generally recognized standard machine finish produced by the planers.

MALPAIS—Literally, badland; refers to dark-colored rock, commonly lava, in rough terrain. As defined for architectural use: calcium carbonate with other components which give it color, markings, and texture suitable as a desirable building stone.

MARBLE—A metamorphic limestone in a more or less crystalline state capable of taking a high polish. Occurs in a wide range of colors and variations. Marble that contains less than five percent magnesium carbonate may be termed calcite marble; from 5 to 40 percent magnesium carbonate, magnesian or dolomitic marble; and more than 40 percent, dolomite marble. These limiting values are, however, not strictly established in petrologic science and are used herein as arbitrary limits.

ONYX—So called in trade, is a crystalline form, commonly microcrystalline, of calcium carbonate deposited usually from cold-water solutions. It is generally translucent and shows a characteristic layering. The term onyx marble is technically a misnomer, as true onyx is a variety of cryptocrystalline fibrous silica (chalcedony), and is closely related in form and origin to agate.

SERPENTINE—A marble characterized by a prominent amount of the mineral serpentine.

TRAVERTINE—A form of limestone precipitated from ground waters, as in caves or in orifices of springs (see Limestone Group).

VERDE ANTIQUE—A commercial marble composed chiefly of massive serpentine and capable of taking a high degree of polish. Verde antique is not a true marble in the scientific sense, but is commonly sold as a decorative commercial marble and requires the adjectival modifier verde(or verd) antique. Verde antique is commonly veined with carbonate minerals, chiefly calcite and dolomite.

MASONRY—Built up construction, usually of a combination of materials set in mortar.

METAMORPHISM—The change or alteration in a rock caused by exterior agencies, such as deep-seated heat and pressure, or intrusion of rock materials.

MITER—The junction of two unites at an angle of which the junction line usually bisects on a 45° angle.

MODULAR MULTIPLE-CUT (PATTERN-CUT)—This refers to standard patterns used throughout the stone industry. These patterns are usually based on multiples of a given height. Stone that is multiple cut or pattern cut is pre-cut to allow typically for ¼'' or ½'' joints or beds.

MOLDINGS—Decorative stone deviating from a plane surface by projections, curved profiles, recesses or any combination thereof.

MORTAR—A plastic mixture of cement, lime, sand, and water used to bond masonry units.

MOSAIC—A veneering which is generally irregular with no definite pattern. Nearly all the stone used in a mosaic pattern is irregular in shape.

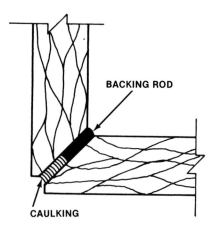

Figure 9-8
45° Miter Joint.

N

NATURAL BED—The setting of the stone on the same plane as it was formed in the ground. This generally applies to all stratified materials.

NATURAL CLEFT—This generally pertains to stones which are formed in layers in the ground. When such stones are cleaved or separated along a natural seam the remaining surface is referred to as a natural cleft surface.

NICKED BIT FINISH—Obtained by planing the stone with a planer tool in which irregular nicks have been made in the cutting edge.

NON-STAINING MORTAR—Mortar composed of materials which individually or collectively do not contain material that will stain. Usually having a very low alkali content.

O

OBSIDIAN—A glassy phase of lava.

ONYX MARBLE—A dense, crystalline form of lime carbonate deposited usually from cold-water solutions. Generally translucent and shows a characteristic layering due to mode of accumulation.

OOLITIC LIMESTONE—A calcite-cemented calcareous stone formed of shells and shell fragments, practically non-crystalline in character. It is found in massive deposits located almost entirely in Lawrence, Monroe, and Owen Counties, Indiana and in Alabama, Kansas, and Texas. This limestone is characteristically a freestone, without cleavage planes, possessing a remarkable uniformity of composition, texture and structure. It possesses a high internal elasticity, adapting itself without damage to extreme temperature changes.

OPALIZED—The introduction into a rock of siliceous material in the form of opal, hydrous silicate.

OUT OF WIND—To be out of wind is to have the arris of the stone not in parallel or perpendicular lines. Stone which is out of wind has an irregular or rustic appearance.

P

PALLETIZED—A system of stacking stone on wooden pallets. Stone which comes palletized is easily moved and transported by modern handling equipment. Palletized stone generally arrives at the job site in better condition than unpalletized material.

PARAPET WALL—That part of any wall entirely above the roof line.

PARGING—Plastering a cementitious coating of mortar onto a surface, often used for damp-proofing.

PARQUETRY—An inlay of stone floors in geometrical or other patterns.

PERFORATED WALL—One which contains a considerable number of relatively small openings. Often called pierced wall or screen wall.

PERRONS—Slabs of stone set on other stones serving as steps and arches in gardens.

PHENOCRYST—In igneous rocks, the relatively large and conspicuous crystals in a finer-grained matrix or ground mass.

PILASTER—An engaged pier of shallow depth; in classical architecture it follows the height and width of related columns, with similar base and cap.

PITCHED STONE—Stone having arris clearly defined; face, however, is roughly cut with pitching chisel used along the line which becomes the arris.

PLINTHS—The lower square part of the base of a column. A square base or a lower block, as of a pedestal. The base block at the juncture of baseboard and trim around an opening.

PLUCKED FINISH—Obtained by rough-planing the surface of stone, breaking or plucking out small particles to give rough texture.

POINTING—The filling and tooling of mortar joints with mortar or caulking compounds.

POLISHED—The finest and smoothest finish available in stone characterized by a gloss or reflective property. Generally only possible on hard, dense materials.

PORPHYRY—An igneous rock in which relatively large and conspicuous crystals (phenocrysts) are set in a matrix of finer crystals.

PRESSURE RELIEVING JOINT—An open horizontal joint below the supporting angle or hanger located at approximately every floor line and not over 15 feet apart horizontally and every 20 to 30 feet vertically to prevent the weight from being transmitted to the masonry below. These joints are to be caulked with a resilient non-staining material to prevent moisture penetration.

PROJECTIONS—This refers to the pulling out of stones in a wall to give an effect of ruggedness. The amount of each stone is pulled out can vary between ½'' and 1½''. Stones are either pulled out at the same degree at both ends or sometimes one end is pulled out, leaving the other end flush with the majority of veneer.

PUMICE—An exceptionally cellular, glassy lava resembling a solid froth.

Q

QUARRY—An excavation where usable stone is extracted from the ground.

QUARTZ—A silicon dioxide mineral that occurs in colorless and transparent or colored hexagonal crystals and also in crystalline masses. One of the most common minerals, the chief constituent of sandstone.

QUARTZITE—A compact granular rock composed of quartz crystals, usually so firmly cemented as to make the mass homogeneous. The stone is generally quarried in stratified layers, the surfaces of which are unusually smooth. Its crushing and tensile strengths are extremely high; the color range is wide.

QUARTZITIC SANDSTONE—A sandstone with a high concentration of quartz grains and siliceous cement.

QUIRT—A groove separating a bed or other moulding from the adjoining members.

QUOINS—Stones at the corner of a wall emphasized by size, projection, rustification, or by a different finish.

R

RANGE—A course of any thickness that is continued across the entire face. All range courses need not be of the same thickness.

RECESS—A sinkage in a wall plane.

REGLET—A recess used to receive and secure flashing.

RELIEF or **RELIEVE**—Ornament in relief. The ornament or figure can be slightly, half, or greatly projected.

RELIEVING ARCH—One built over a lintel, flat arch or smaller arch to divert loads, thus relieving the lower member from excessive loading. Also known as discharging or safety arch.

RETURN—The right angle turn of a molding.

RETURN HEAD—Stone facing with the finish appearing on both the face and the edge of the same stone, as on the corner of a building.

REVEAL—The depth of stone between its outer face and a window or door set in an opening.

RIFT—The most pronounced (see GRAIN) direction of splitting or cleavage of a stone. Rift and grain may be obscure, as in some granites, but are important in both quarrying and processing stone.

RIPRAP—Irregular shaped stones used for facing bridge abutments and fills. Stones thrown together without order to form a foundation or sustaining walls.

RISE—The word "rise" refers to the heights of stone. Generally used in reference to veneer stone.

ROCK—An integral part of the earth's crust composed of an aggregate of grains of one or more minerals. (Stone is the commercial term applied to quarry products.)

ROCK (PITCH) FACE—This is similar to split face, except that the face of the stone is pitched to a given line and plane producing a bold appearance rather than the comparatively straight face obtained in split face.

RODDING—Reinforcement of a structurally unsound marble by cementing reinforcing rods into grooves or channels cut into the back of the slab.

ROMAN ARCH—Semi-circular arch.

Figure 9–9
Roman arch.

ROSE WINDOW—A circular stone window fitted with carved tracery.

ROUGH SAWN—A marble surface finish accomplished by the gang sawing process.

RUBBED FINISH—Mechanically rubbed for smoother finish.

RUBBLE—A product term applied to dimension stone used for building purposes, chiefly walls and foundations, and consisting of irregularly shaped pieces, partly trimmed or squared, generally with one split or finished face, and selected and specified with a size range.

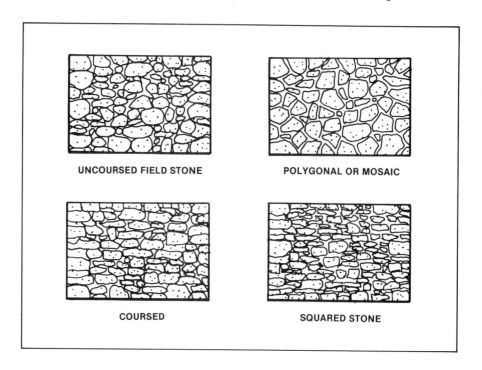

UNCOURSED FIELD STONE

POLYGONAL OR MOSAIC

COURSED

SQUARED STONE

Figure 9–10
Rubble masonry.

RUSTICATION—Chamfers or square sinkings round the face edges of individual stones to create shadows and to give an appearance of greater weight to the lower part of a building. When only the horizontal joints are sunk, the device is known as banded rustication.

RUSTIFICATION—Recessing the margin of cut stone so that when placed together a channel is formed at each joint.

S

SADDLE—A flat strip of stone projecting above the floor between the jambs of a door; a threshold.

SANDBLASTED—A dull non-glossy finish applied to stone; usually accomplished by blasting air blended with sand across the surface.

SAND-SAWN FINISH—The surface left as the stone comes from the gang saw. Moderately smooth, granular surface varying with the texture and grade of stone.

SANDSTONE—A sedimentary rock consisting usually of quartz cemented with silica, iron oxide or calcium carbonate. Sandstone is durable, has a very high crushing and tensile strength, and a wide range of colors and textures.

Varieties of sandstone are commonly designated by the kind and prominence of interstitial and bonding materials, as siliceous sandstone (bonding material primarily silica), calcareous sandstone (calcium carbonate prominent as bonding material or as accessory grains or both), argillaceous sandstone (clay minerals prominent as interstitial or bonding materials, or as thin laminac), ferruginous sandstone (iron oxide or hydroxide minerals, or as thin laminac), ferruginous sandstone (iron oxide or hydroxide minerals (hematic, limonite, et al) as interstitial or as bonding materials in sufficient amount to impart appreciable color to the stone): brownstone (ferruginous sandstone of dark brown or reddish brown color), arkose, arkosic sandstone, or feldspathic sandstone (a sandstone that contains an abundance of grains of feldspar), conglomerate (a sandstone composed in large part of rounded pebbles, also called puddingstone).

The term "brownstone" was applied originally to certain Trassic sandstones of the Connecticut Valley in Massachusetts (Longmeadow sandstone), Connecticut (Portland sandstone), and to similarly appearing reddish-brown sandstone quarried in and near Hummelstown, Pennsylvania. Thus the term originally had geographic significance, but such geographic limitation is undesirable.

SAWED EDGE—A clean cut edge generally achieved by cutting with a diamond blade, gang saw or wire saw.

SAWED FACE—A finish obtained from the process used in producing building stone. Varies in texture from smooth to rough and coincident with the type of materials used in sawing; characterized as diamond sawn, sand sawn, chat sawn, and shot sawn.

SCALE—Thin lamina or paper-like sheets of rock, often loose, and interrupting an otherwise smooth surface on stone.

SCHIST—A loose term applying to foliated metamorphic rock (recrystallized) characterized by thin foliae that are composed predominantly of minerals of thin platy or prismatic habits and whose long dimensions are oriented in approximately parallel positions along the planes of foliation. Because of this foliated structure schists split readily along these planes and so possess a pronounced rock cleavage. The more common schists are composed of the micas and other mica-like minerals (such as chlorite) and generally contain subordinate quartz and/or feldspar of comparatively fine-grained texture; all graduations exist between schist and gneiss (coarsely foliated feldspathic rocks).

SCORIA—Irregular masses of lava resembling clinker of slag; may be cellular (vesicular) dark-colored and heavy.

SCOTIA—A concave molding.

SCULPTURE—Statuary cut from stone by a sculptor using hand tools and polishing materials.

SEMI-RUBBED—A finish achieved by rubbing by hand or machine the rough or high spots off the surface to be used leaving a certain amount of the natural surface along with the smoothed areas.

SERPENTINE—a hydrous magnesium silicate material of igneous origin, generally a very dark green color with markings of white, light green or black. One of the hardest varieties of natural building stone.

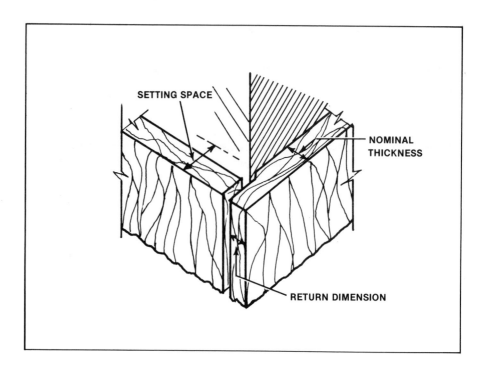

Figure 9-11
Setting space.

SETTING SPACE—A term used to indicate the distance from the finished face of the marble to the face of the backup wall.

SHEAR—A type of stress; a body is in shear when it is subjected to a pair of equal forces which are opposite in direction and which act along parallel planes.

SHOT-SAWN—Description of a finish obtained by using steel shot in the gang sawing process to produce random markings for a rough surface texture.

SHOT-SAWN FINISH—A rough gang-saw finish produced by sawing with chilled steel shot.

SILL—A flat stone used under windows, doors, and other masonry openings.

SILTSTONE—A fine-grained non-carbonate clastic rock composed of at least 67 percent of detrital grains of quartz and silicate minerals of silt size. Siltstones are rarely marketed as such but commonly are considered as fine-grained sandstones. This class of sediments is texturally transitional between sandstones and shales (mudstones). Many bluestones and siliceous flagstones fall within this category. The term is included in these definitions chiefly to explain the relationship of some siliceous flagstones to the sandstone category.

SLAB—A lengthwise cut of a large quarry block of stone.

SLATE—A very fine-grained metamorphic rock derived from sedimentary rock shale. Characterized by an excellent parallel cleavage entirely independent of original bedding, by which cleavage the rock may be split easily into relatively thin slabs.

Essential mineral constituents of slates are usually members of the mica group, commonly sericite, muscovite, and paragonite; of the clay group, chiefly illite and kaolinite; and of the chlorite group. Common accessory minerals are iron oxides, calcite, quarts, and feldspar. Other minerals may be present also as minor accessories. Most slates are derived from shales. Others are derived from fine-grained igneous rock, chiefly volcanic tuffs, but these are rare and of little commercial importance.

SLIP SILL—A stone sill set between the jambs. (See LUG SILL.)

SMOOTH FINISH—Description of the finish produced by planer machines plus the removal of objectionable tool marks. Also known as ''smooth planer finish'' and ''smooth machine finish.''

SNAPPED EDGE, QUARRY CUT or BROKEN EDGE—This generally refers to a natural breaking of a stone either by hand or machine. The break should be at right angles to the top and bottom surface.

SOAPSTONE—A massive variety of talc with a soapy or greasy feel used for hearths, washtubs, table tops, carved ornaments, chemical laboratories, etc., known for its stain-proof qualities.

SOFFIT—The finished, exposed underside of a lintel, arch, or portico.

SPALL—A stone fragment that has split or broken off.

SPALLS—Sizes may vary from chip-size to one- and two-man stones. Spalls are primarily used for taking up large voids in rough rubble or mosaic patterns.

SPANDREL WALL—That part of a curtain wall above the top of a window in one story and below the sill of the window in the story above.

SPLAY—A beveled or slanted surface.

SPLINE—A thin strip of material, such as wood or metal, inserted into the edges of two stone pieces or stone tiles to make a butt joint between them.

SPLIT—Division of a rock by cleavage.

SPLIT FACE (SAWED BED)—Usually split face is sawed on the beds and is split either by hand or with machine so that the surface face of the stone exhibits the natural quarry texture.

SPLITSTONE FINISH—Obtained by sawing to accurate heights then breaking by machine to required bed widths. (Normal bed widths are 3½''.)

SPOT OR SPOTTING—An adhesive contact, usually of plaster of paris, applied between the back of marble veneer and the face of the backup wall to plumb or secure standing marble.

STACKED BOND—Stone that is cut to one dimension and installed with unbroken vertical and horizontal joints running the entire length and height of the veneered area.

STATUE—A sculpture of a human or animal figure.

STICKING—Trade language for connecting pieces of stone together by using cement or epoxies.

STONE—Sometimes synonymous with rock, but more properly applied to individual blocks, masses or fragments taken from their original formation or considered for commercial use.

STOOL—A flat stone, generally polished, used as an interior sill.

STRATIFICATION—A structure produced by deposition of sediments in beds or layers (strata), laminae, lenses, wedges, and other essentially tabular units.

STRIP RUBBLE—Generally speaking, strip rubble comes from a lege quarry. The beds of the stone, while uniformly straight, are of the natural cleft as the stone is removed from the ledge, and then split by machine to approximately four inch widths.

STRIPS—Long pieces of stone, usually low height ashlar courses, where length to height ratio is at maximum for the material used.

STYOLITE—A longitudinally streaked, columnar structure occurring in some marbles and of the same material as the marble in which it occurs.

SURROUNG—An enframement.

T

TABLET—A small, flat slab or surface of stone, especially one bearing or intended to bear an inscription, carving or the like.

TEMPLATE—(1) A pattern for repetitive marking or fabricating operation. (2) "Safe" a water closet base.

TERRAZZO—A type of concrete in which chips or pieces of stone, usually marble, are mixed with cement and are ground to a flat surface, exposing the chips, which take a high polish.

THIN STONE—Stone slabs generally of two inches or less in thickness.

TOLERANCE—Dimensional allowance made for the inability of men and machines to fabricate a product of exact dimensions.

THROAT—The name sometimes given to the small groove under a window sill or dripstone intended to deflect rain water from the wall face.

TOOLED FINISH—Customarily are four, six or eight parallel, concave grooves to the inch.

TRACERY—Ornamentation of panels, circular windows, window heads, etc.

TRANSLUCENCE—Permitting light to pass through with little diffusing. Certain marble varieties are translucent.

TRAVERTINE LIMESTONE—A variety of limestone that has a partly crystaline or microcrystaline texture and porous or cellular layered structure, the cells being usually concentrated along certain layers and commonly displaying small stalactitic forms.

TRAVERTINE MARBLE—A variety of limestone regarded as a product of chemical precipitation from hot springs. Travertine is cellular with the cells usually concentrated in thin layers that display a stalactitic structure. Some that take a polish are sold as marble and may be classified as travertine marble under the class of "Commercial Marble."

TREAD—A flat stone used as the top walking surface on steps.

TRIM—Stone used as decorative items only, such as sills, coping, enframements, etc., with the facing of another material.

TRIMMER ARCH—A stone arch, usually a low-rise arch, used for supporting a fireplace hearth.

TUFF—Cemented volcanic ash, many varieties included.

U

UNDERCUT—Cut so as to present an overhanging part.

V

VEIN CUT—Cutting quarried marble or stone perpendicular to the natural bedding plane.

VEININGS—Colored markings in limestone, marble, alabaster, etc.

VENEER STONE—Any stone used as a decorative facing material which is not meant to be load-bearing.

VENTING—Creating an outlet in a wall for air and moisture to pass through. (See CAVITY VENT.)

VERD (or VERDE) ANTIQUE—A marble composed chiefly of massive serpentine and capable of being polished. It is commonly crossed by veinlets of other minerals, chiefly carbonates of calcium and magnesium.

VUG—A cavity in rock, sometimes lined or filled with either amorphous or crystalline material, common in calcereous rocks such as marble or limestone.

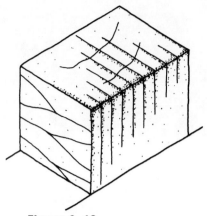

Figure 9–12
Vein cut.

W

WALL PLATE—A horizontal member anchored to a masonry wall to which other structural elements may be attached. Also called HEAD PLATE.

WALLS—(1) BEARING: A wall supporting a vertical load in addition to its own weight.

(2) CAVITY: A wall in which the inner and outer wythes are separated by an air space, but tied together with metal ties.

(3) COMPOSITE: A wall in which the facing and backing are of different materials and bonded together with bond stones to exert a common reaction under load.

(4) VENEER or FACED: A wall in which a thin facing and the backing are of different materials, but not so bonded as to exert a common reaction under load.

(5) WIND (WINED): A twisting warp from cutting slabs in the gang saws.

(6) WYTHE: The inner or outer part of a cavity wall.

WALL TIE—A bonder or metal piece which connects wythes of masonry to each other or to other materials.

WALL TIE CAVITY—A rigid, corrosion-resistant metal tie which bonds two wythes of a cavity wall. It is usually steel, 3/16'' in diameter and formed in a ''Z'' shape or a rectangle.

WARPED WALLS—Generally a condition experienced only in flagging or flagstone materials; very common with flagstone materials that are taken from the ground and used in their natural state. To eliminate warping in stones it would be necessary to further finish the material, such as machining, sand rubbing, honing, or polishing.

WASH—A sloped area or the area water will run over.

WATER BAR—Typically a strip in a reglet in window sill and stone below to prevent water passage.

WATER TABLE—A projection of lower masonry on the outside of the wall slightly above the ground. Often a damp course is placed at the level of the water table to prevent upward penetration of ground water.

WAXING—An expression used in the marble finishing trade to indicate the filling of natural voids with color-blended materials.

WEAR—The removal of material or impairment of surface finish through friction or impact use.

WEATHERING—(1) Natural alteration by either chemical or mechanical processes due to the action of constituents of the atmosphere, surface waters, soil and other ground waters, or to temperature changes.
(2) The inclined top surface of a stone such as a coping, cornice, or window sill.

WEDGING—Splitting of stone by driving wedges into planes of weakness.

WEEP HOLES—Openings placed in mortar joints of facing material at the level of flashing to permit the escape of moisture.

WIRE SAW—A method of cutting stone by passing a twisted, multistrand wire over the stone and immersing the wire in a slurry of abrasive material.

Bibliography

Amrhein, James E., et al. Masonry Design Manual. Los Angeles: Masonry Industry Advancement Committee, 1979.

Amrhein, James E., Hatch, Robert, Merrigan, Michael. Anchored Stone Veneer Test Report. Los Angeles, California: Masonry Institute of America, 1989.

Beall, Christine. Masonry Design and Detailing for Architects, Engineers, and Builders. Englewood Cliffs, N.J.: Prentice-Hall Inc., 1984.

Borchelt, J. Gregg. Construction Tolerances and Design Consideration for Masonry Veneer and Structural Frames: Proceedings of the Third North American Masonry Conference, 1985. Third Canadian Masonry Symposium.

Borchelt, J. Gregg and Larry G. Griffis and James F. Richardson. Stone Cladding: Connection Design. Third Canadian Masonry Symposium.

Building Stone Institute. Stone Catalog. New York, New York: B.S.I., 1978.

Canadian Standards Association. Connectors for Masonry. Rexdale, Ontario, Canada: CSA, 1984.

Catani, Mario J. Protection of Embedded Steel in Masonry. Construction Specifier, 1985.

Clifton, James R. Stone Consolidating Materials—A Status Report. Washington, D.C.: National Bureau of Standards, 1980.

Clifton-Taylor, Alec, and A. S. Ireson. English Stone Building. Hampshire, England: BAS Printers Limited, 1983.

Engineering News Record. Buildings are Turning to Stone. ENR, March 1984.

Gere, Alex S. "Recommended Practices For The Use of Natural Stones In Building Construction." Building Stone Magazine, May/June 1981.

Grimm, Clayford T. University of Texas at Austin.

Indiana Limestone Institute of America. The Finishing Touch. Bedford, Indiana: ILI, 1979.

International Conference of Building Officials. Dwelling Construction Under the Uniform Building Code. Whittier, California: ICBO, 1985.

International Conference of Building Officials. Uniform Building Code. Whittier, California: ICBO, 1985.

International Masonry Institute. The Masonry Glossary. Boston, Massachusetts: CBI Publishing Comapny, Inc., 1981.

Italian Marble Industrie, The. A Technical Guide to the Rational Use of Marble. Milano, Italy: Rizzoli Grafica, 1972.

Marble Institute of America. Marble Design Manual II. Farmington, MI: MIA, 1983.

Masonry Institute of America. Marble Veneer. Los Angeles: MIA, 1976.

McDonald, W. H. How to Avoid and Remove Small Area Stains and Blemishes. Indiana Limestone Design and Procedure Aids. Bedford, Indiana: Indiana Limestone Institute.

Schneider, Robert R. and Walter L. Dickey. Reinforced Masonry Design. Englewood Cliffs, N.J.: Prentice-Hall Inc., 1980.

Torraca, Giorgio. Porous Building Materials. Rome, Italy: International Centre for the Study of the Preservation and the Restoration of Cultural Property, 1982.

Torraca, Giorgio. Solubility and Solvents for Conservation Problems Rome, Italy: Centre for the Study of the Preservation and the Restoration of Cultural Property, 1978.

Vermont Marble Company. Marble Color Selector and Use Guide. Proctor, Vermont: VMC, 1971.